THE PREPOSITION BOOK

PRACTICE TOWARD MASTERING ENGLISH PREPOSITIONS

Tom Cole
Arizona State University

Ann Arbor
THE UNIVERSITY OF MICHIGAN PRESS

ISBN-13: 978-0-472-03166-5
ISBN-10: 0-472-03166-X

Published in the United States of America
The University of Michigan Press

Manufactured in the United States of America

♻ Printed on acid-free paper

2009   2008   2007   2006   4   3   2   1

Contents

Chapter 2   Prepositions for Daily Life and the Classroom   30

Part C Explanations   9–13

Part D Explanations   14–18

Chapter 5   Prepositions for Viewing the World, Narrating Trips and Vacations, and Describing Emotions   130

Part I Explanations   39–43

Chapter 7   Prepositions for Exemplifying and Comparing/Contrasting   195

Part N Explanations *68–74*

An Important Note Regarding the Organization of the Text

When I decided to put together a text on prepositions, I first had to decide which prepositions would go where. I recognized immediately that the most obvious thing that related prepositions was simple morphology: one-word versus two-word prepositions, for example. I also could see right away that structuring a book according to such groupings would result in more of a dictionary than a useful classroom text.

Organizing an effective class text on prepositions involves finding out how prepositions go together logically, how they match real world use, and how they might relate to the typical ESL classroom and the typical ESL curriculum. Accordingly, this text is first sequenced in accordance with general level of difficulty. Basic-level prepositions like *in, on,* and *at* with place and time come first; higher-level items such as the *by* in passive voice or the preposition *unlike* for showing contrast are presented later on. The early chapters deal with daily life matters suitable for the curriculum of lower-intermediate students, but at the same time they provide a useful review for the most advanced learners. Later chapters build on the ones before to add sophistication to the students' use of prepositions. In addition, the readings go from simple anecdotes to higher intermediate readings, such as short newspaper articles.

Throughout the book, many of the essential points of English grammar and usage so familiar to teachers in the field are continuously practiced along with the prepositions that go hand in hand with them. Also, prepositions and related structures are presented in chapters according to whether they might be germane to description, narration, exemplification, cause and effect, opinion, and comparing and contrasting.

The result is a book on prepositions that simultaneously treats a substantial number of the essential ESL particulars that all teachers present in nearly every class. I believe that this will make the book a good choice as a class text for a number of different courses.

Tom Cole

Introduction

To the Student

How to Learn with The Preposition Book

The Preposition Book has been written to make English prepositions easier to understand and use. If you are studying alone and have questions about certain prepositions, you can check the Contents and study those parts alone. However, prepositions from earlier chapters are included in many exercises later in the book. Therefore, the best method is to start at the beginning and finish the text, completing all of the exercises. Be sure to look at each explanation carefully. Make sure you understand the explanation before you try to do the exercises that follow it.

The Preposition Book gives examples of the most common ways that prepositions are used in English. If you follow the examples in the book, you will almost always be correct. However, no rules of grammar in any language are absolute. Therefore, you shouldn't be surprised if you occasionally find exceptions as you read and listen to English.

The Preposition Book contains a lot of exercises, and it covers a lot of material. There is an answer key at the end of each chapter for all of the numbered exercises and all of the Quick Check exercises. The Putting It Together sections and the Expansion Exercises at the end of each chapter are included to give you extra practice. They have no answer key, so you will want a teacher or a native English speaker to check your work on these exercises to make sure you are not making mistakes.

When you finish a chapter, take the Comprehensive Test and then check your choices in the Key to Comprehensive Tests in the back of the book. The Key to Comprehensive Tests tells you where to find explanations for every question. If you do not get at least 90 percent on a Comprehensive Test, review the chapter again. Reinforce your study of each part of the book by playing the software games every day.

When you have finished all the chapter exercises, don't put the book away—keep it on your desk, ready to use. *The Preposition Book* is a reference that you can use every day to improve your writing and speaking because using the correct prepositions will help you sound more fluent.

To the Teacher

English prepositions are a well-known problem area for new language learners. The reason for this is plain enough: There are a tremendous number of prepositional combinations in English, and they seldom seem to follow any rules. While the typical ESL curriculum for beginners almost always includes a solid prepositional component, intermediate and advanced students often get less and less instruction with these forms. As important as they are, prepositions are not often the logical sub-focus of the major grammatical structures that teachers teach. The result is that students pick up what they can of prepositions along the way but remain weak in this area—and they are often quite aware of this weakness.

The Preposition Book is intended as a resource, guide, and workbook to address students' questions and misconceptions regarding English prepositions. The text is as comprehensive as it is practical and treats beginning to advanced prepositional usage. However, the exercises included are not intended for beginning students. The text was written at an *intermediate level* to make it useful to the greatest number of students.

The Preposition Book relies on short explanations of each preposition or group of prepositions. These numbered explanations are often accompanied by charts, pictures, sentences, and word lists. The explanations exist to provide a logical framework for the text and to serve as a handy reference. Learning of prepositions takes place principally through guided practice that often includes a solid context.

The Preposition Book contains numerous simple assignments entitled **Putting It Together**, which are designed to make the book easy to use as a classroom text because they can be done as a classroom activity or assigned as homework for a class. Finally, **Expansion Exercises** offer simple suggestions for extra homework practice, and **Comprehensive Tests** with answers keyed to the explanations provide a final progress check at the end of each chapter. Keys to comprehensive tests are found at the end of the book.

The Preposition Book also comes packaged with three software games to reinforce each explanation. The software makes it easy to assign homework that focuses on any part of the book. Teachers need only tell the students to play a game for any chapter, part, or combination of parts and print out their results. Students can also be asked to take a test on any chapter or any combination of parts and bring their scores to class. The software generates paper tests for any chapter or any combination of parts.

How to Learn Using *The Preposition Book* Software *(Preposition Pinball and Other Games)*

Getting the Most from the Software

Special effort has been taken to create the intuitive interface of *The Preposition Book's* software, which makes it possible to use the software immediately without ever having to consult a manual.

Just by clicking the buttons, students and teachers should quickly understand how the software operates whether they are playing one of the games, taking a test, getting material from the Library pages, or doing anything else in the program. Students working in a lab can be asked to start the program, and typically with no further direction they will soon be involved in the game and learning about prepositions.

To get the most from *Preposition Pinball and Other Games* software, however, we offer some tips and ideas that can help bring the power of the computer to bear on both learning and instructing. What appears here is what can be considered the software's manual. The rules of play and explanations of features in the program are described in the form of FAQs. Tips and ideas useful to both students and teachers are also provided.

Rules of Play

FAQ: What are the rules of play?

Answer:

1. **Five Palms Preposition Pinball**

   As in most pinball games, the game starts with five balls and is over when all the balls have been lost. One ball is lost for each incorrect answer, and one palm tree disappears from the screen at the same time. If the user is doing well, however, the game gives back balls and palm trees from time to time and the game can continue indefinitely. Bonus points are awarded randomly.

2. **Carp Derby**

   The user catches a small fish with each correct answer but loses one of the three large fish with each two mistakes. After six mistakes, the game usually ends, but if the player begins to do well for an extended period, the large fish are given back and the game can continue indefinitely.

3. **Diamond Mine**

   The user finds diamonds with each correct answer but loses one of three mining picks with each two mistakes. After six mistakes, the game usually ends, but if the player begins to do well for an extended period, the mining picks are given back and the game can continue indefinitely. Red diamonds are worth $5,000, blue ones $1,000, green ones $500, and yellow ones $100. A total profit tally is continually updated.

Presentation of Material

FAQ: How is the material presented?

Answer: There are hundreds of questions, and all are presented randomly. The software will never repeat the same question until all items have been used up. In addition, there is always an option for an on-the-fly explanation for any item, and players can see mistakes and scores for the current session at any time.

The players also have a great deal of control over what material is practiced. It is possible to practice a single part of *The Preposition Book* or combine up to seven parts at once. Any combination is allowed. This makes the software appropriate for beginners and very advanced students alike.

FAQ: Do the games exactly match the parts in The Preposition Book by letter?

<u>Answer</u>: Yes.

FAQ: If I don't understand why my answer is wrong, what do I do?

<u>Answer</u>: Just click the Why button if you have any questions. You will be sent to the rule that explains the preposition in the sentence. The number of the rule will have a square around it. If you don't immediately see the exact explanation of your sentence, just scroll down a few lines. Clicking the Why button is an important part of learning with software.

FAQ: What is the GO button on the two type-in games for?

<u>Answer</u>: The type-in games (Carp Derby and Diamond Mine) are designed to be easy to use for touch typists. The GO button does the job of the RETURN or ENTER key on your keyboard. Clicking it will return your cursor to the typing field if it has ever moved and will give you a new question if you need one. Usually, however, just typing answers and hitting RETURN or ENTER are all you need to play the game.

FAQ: How do I turn the sound on and off?

<u>Answer</u>: On the screen for each game is a musical staff (&) button. Click it to turn the sound on and off.

Testing

FAQ: How does the Make a Test! button on the Main Menu work?

<u>Answer</u>: Just click the Make a Test! button on the Main Menu for complete directions. The tests are generated with random questions from any chapter or part of the book you select. It's easy to print out a neat 15-, 20-, or 30-point class test with this feature, and no test is ever exactly the same.

FAQ: How do you use the testing component in the software?

<u>Answer</u>: There is always an option for a 20-point quiz in any of the three games. Learners simply click the **Take a Test** button anytime during play. Each test is automatically corrected and graded. The carefully corrected test shows exactly how the student answered and which answer or answers are correct. All completed tests are immediately available for printing or viewing on the game page and ALWAYS accessible from the main menu by clicking **View My Tests**. All test results are also recorded with the game scores, which are accessible by clicking the **Records** button on the current game screen or on the Main Menu.

FAQ: Can learners print out customized tests that focus on the areas with which they need the most practice?

<u>Answer</u>: Absolutely. Since the software records every mistake the users make, these sentences can be printed out as custom-made quizzes that focus on the very aspects of article use that each student needs the most practice with. They can also be printed out as study sheets with the answers included.

To view and print mistakes, students simply click the **Records** button (on the current game screen or the Main Menu) and choose the mistakes option. To print out a custom-made quiz, students print the mistakes without the answers. To create a study sheet, students print out their mistakes with the answers included.

Here is a step-by-step procedure for teachers who are working with students in a lab and want to create study sheets and custom-made quizzes for their students:

1. Have the students play a game.

2. After they have played, ask them to stop and click the **Records** button for the game. (They can also access these records from the Main Menu.) The students will have the option to see their scores and test results or their mistakes.

3. To print a study sheet, the students simply print their mistakes with the answers included. (Have them click the **Answers** button to include the answers with the list of mistakes.) For custom-made quizzes, students print their mistakes without the answers. In either case, the students should be instructed to click the **Number** button to get a neat, numbered print-out. The software also requires students to enter their names whenever they print their mistakes, so in a lab setting it is conveniently clear whose quiz or study sheet is whose.

Records

FAQ: Does the software record every mistake that is made?

<u>Answer</u>: Yes, automatically—and it always gives the user the option to record all game and test scores as well.

FAQ: Does the software keep a record of my work after I quit the program?

<u>Answer</u>: No. The software reverts to its original state each time it is launched. This fresh start is especially important in a lab setting. Take a moment to print your test results, mistakes, and game scores whenever you wish, or copy them to the clipboard and paste them into any word processing document. Remember, you can print or copy any data you see in the software.

Library

FAQ: Where are all of the questions? Can I see them all at the same time?

<u>Answer</u>: Yes! Just click the **Library** button on the Main Menu. You will be sent to the Preposition Library and Archives page. There you can see every question from every Part (A–N) of the software. Just choose a part to see all of its questions. From this screen, you can also access your records and all of the explanations used in the software. On the Library page, you even can view and print the seven tests from the book along with their answer keys.

Technical Stuff

FAQ: I have a Macintosh. Is the Windows version of the software different?

<u>Answer</u>: No. The software is the same whether you have a Windows or a Macintosh machine.

FAQ: How do you install the software?

<u>Answer</u>: There is no installation process aside from copying the program to your hard drive. Just copy the software program from the CD to your desktop. Double-clicking its icon will launch the program.

FAQ: How do I uninstall the software?

<u>Answer</u>: Just drag it into the trash and empty the trash (Macintosh), or drag it into the recycle bin and empty the recycle bin (Windows).

Ordering Information

FAQ: How do I order additional copies of the software?

<u>Answer</u>: On the main Menu, click the **Ordering** button.

What Is a Preposition?

If you buy this book, sooner or later someone will ask you, "What is a preposition?" As a student of English, you can probably already answer with something like this: "Prepositions are little words like *in, on,* and *at.* They are very important to the meaning of a sentence, and they can be difficult for people who are learning English."

Your definition is good enough. It is much clearer than the definition you will find in the dictionary, and it answers the question better. Don't change it. Instead, expand your knowledge of prepositions by considering the following about prepositions.

1. A preposition usually goes before a noun or noun phrase (a noun and the words that go with it).

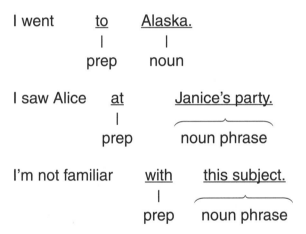

2. A preposition sometimes consists of more than one word.

I walked <u>across</u> the street.	one-word preposition
Shannon lives <u>next to</u> the fire station.	two-word preposition
<u>In spite of</u> the rain, we went on a picnic.	three-word preposition

3. A preposition sometimes seems logical.

   Most people come to work <u>in</u> their cars.

4. A preposition sometimes seems illogical.

   I came here <u>on</u> the bus. (You are really in or inside the bus and not on or on top of it.)

5. A preposition is sometimes optional.

   When I'm <u>at</u> home, I feel safe.   Correct

   When I'm home, I feel safe.   Correct

6. A preposition is needed in some sentences.

   The men went <u>to</u> work.   Correct

   The men went work.   *Incorrect*

7. A preposition may not be needed in some types of sentences.

   I went home.   Correct

   I went to home.   *Incorrect*

8. A preposition sometimes can be replaced by a synonym.

   I live <u>near</u> you.

   I live <u>close to</u> you.

9. Like other words in English, a preposition sometimes has an antonym.

   Jane walked <u>into</u> the room and then walked <u>out</u>.

   Why are the lights <u>on</u>? They should be <u>off</u>.

10. A preposition sometimes appears with an adjective.

    good <u>at</u>

    tired <u>of</u>

    harmful <u>to</u>

11. A preposition sometimes appears with a verb.

   borrow <u>from</u>

   talk <u>to</u>

   leave <u>for</u>

12. A preposition is sometimes related to the grammar of a sentence.

I haven't seen you <u>since</u> last year.	perfect tense
The book was written <u>by</u> Mark Twain.	passive voice
She won't graduate <u>until</u> June.	negative idea

13. Some words look exactly like prepositions but are called particles. For example, the word *up* can be a preposition or a particle.

A. I walked <u>up</u> the stairs.	<u>up</u> is a preposition
B. I called <u>up</u> a friend.	<u>up</u> is a particle

   Why is *up* a particle in sentence B but a preposition in sentence A? People who study grammar might say that *up* in the first sentence is related to the noun phrase *the stairs*. Therefore, they say it is a preposition. They might say that *up* in sentence B is related to the verb *call* and therefore is a particle. But ESL students don't need to worry about this difference very much. Learning the difference between particles and prepositions is not as important as learning how to use them both correctly. Therefore, *The Preposition Book* does not focus on the grammatical difference between particles and prepositions. Instead, the two are taught together.

14. The word *up* in the sentences that follow is not technically a preposition, but it looks exactly the same. Particles like *up* in two-word and multiword verbs (also called **phrasal verbs**) often need to be in the correct place in the sentence.

Call <u>up</u> Johnny.	Correct
Call Johnny <u>up</u>.	Correct
Call him <u>up</u>.	Correct
Call up him.	*Incorrect*

15. A preposition (or a particle) sometimes completely changes the meaning of a word.

Two-Word Verb	Meaning
call off	to cancel
call on	to ask a student to answer in class
call up	to telephone

What have you done <u>for</u> us? (something good)

What have you done <u>to</u> us?   (something very bad)

OK, stop. Now, you know enough about what prepositions are. Start Chapter 1 and practice using prepositions.

Prepositions for Daily Life

PART A   Explanations 1–4

One-Word Prepositions: *in, on, at* with Time

Read the explanation, and study the examples. Complete the exercises that follow.

> **Explanation 1:** The prepositions <u>in</u>, <u>on</u>, and <u>at</u> are used to tell about time. Use <u>in</u> for months and years, <u>on</u> for days, and <u>at</u> for clock times.
>
> Mrs. Johnson was born <u>in</u> June. (<u>in</u> 1960, <u>on</u> January 7th, <u>at</u> six o'clock, etc.)

Exercise A1

Fill in the blanks with the correct prepositions according to Explanation 1.

1. Thomas Jefferson died _____ July 4, 1826.

2. Lunch is usually served _____ 12:00 noon.

3. I was born _____ August.

4. Thanksgiving is always celebrated _____ a Thursday.

5. What do American children do _____ Halloween?

6. Everyone knows what happened _____ 1492.

Putting It Together

Review Explanation 1, and answer the questions according to the cues. You may use your real birthday or choose from the birthdays, years, and times provided.

| July | 5:00 in the morning | July 20 | July 20, 1976 | 1976 |

When were you born?

1. (month only) _____

2. (year only) _____

3. (month and day only) _____

4. (month, day, and year) _____

5. (clock time) _____

One-Word Prepositions: *in, on, at* with Place

Read the explanation, and study the examples. Complete the exercises that follow.

> **Explanation 2:** The prepositions <u>in</u>, <u>on</u>, and <u>at</u> are used to tell about places.
>
> **Use <u>in</u> for enclosed spaces.**
>
> The paper is <u>in</u> the box.
> or <u>in</u> the corner of a room (but <u>on</u> or <u>at</u> for streetcorners), <u>in</u> the building, <u>in</u> the wastebasket, etc.
>
> **Use <u>on</u> when something rests on a surface.**
>
> What is <u>on</u> the desk?
> <u>on</u> the table, <u>on</u> the floor, <u>on</u> the mountain, etc.

EXCEPTION TO EXPLANATION 2: Objects rest <u>on</u> <u>chairs</u>, but people sit <u>in</u> <u>chairs</u>.

There is a book <u>on</u> the <u>chair</u>.

All of the students are <u>in</u> their <u>chairs</u>.

Use <u>at</u> for addresses.

I live <u>at</u> 1414 Elm Street.

Use <u>on</u> for streets, roads, boulevards, avenues, drives, lanes, etc.

The bookstore is <u>on</u> Fifth Street.

<u>on</u> Ninth Avenue, <u>on</u> Cherry Lane, etc.

Use <u>on</u> or <u>at</u> for street corners.

We live <u>on</u> the corner of Fifth and Elm.

or

We live <u>at</u> the corner of Fifth and Elm.

Exercise A2

Fill in the blanks with the correct prepositions according to Explanation 2.

1. I live _____ 2015 Sierra Vista Drive.

2. There is a radio tower _____ the mountain.

3. There are three apples _____ that box.

4. The Johnsons bought a house _____ 22nd Avenue.

5. Our shop is located _____ the corner of Linsey and York.

6. Plug in this radio. There's an outlet _____ the corner.

7. When all the students were _____ their chairs, the test began.

8. Our class meets _____ the Henry Fenway Building.

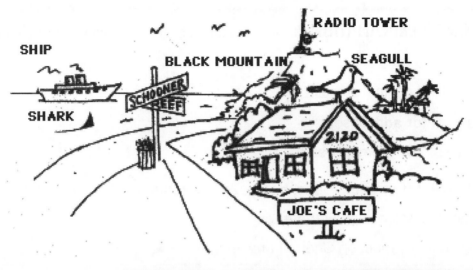

Putting It Together

Review Explanation 2. Answer the questions about the illustration using complete sentences.

1. Where is the ship?

   _____

2. Where is the radio tower?

   _____

3. Where is Joe's Cafe?

   _____

4. Where are the customers?

   _____

5. Where is the trash can?

   _____

6. Where is the trash?

   _____

7. Where is the seagull?

   _____

8. Where is the shark?

   _____

Exercise A3

Review the birth certificate, and answer the questions that follow by writing a preposition in each blank.

OFFICIAL SEAL

St. Joseph Hospital
3126 Hawk Road
Louisville, Kentucky 40201

This certifies that <u>Heather Nelson</u> was born to <u>Emily Price Nelson</u> and <u>John Nelson</u> in this hospital at <u>4:26 AM</u> on Monday, the <u>15th</u> day of <u>July</u>, <u>1978</u>.

In witness whereof the said hospital has caused this certificate to be signed by its duly authorized officer and its official seal to be hereunto affixed.

Sebastian C. Long
Attending Physician

Anna Fields, R.N
Superintendent

1. Where was Heather born? She was born _____ St. Joseph Hospital.

2. What is the year of Heather's birth? She was born _____ 1978.

3. What is the month of Heather's birth? She was born _____ July.

4. What day of the week was it? She was born _____ a Monday.

5. What time was it? She was born _____ 4:26 AM.

6. What is the exact date of Heather's birth? She was born _____ July 15, 1978.

7. Where is St. Joseph Hospital?   It's _____ Hawk Road.

8. What is its complete street address?   It's located _____ 3126 Hawk Road.

One-Word Prepositions: *beside, by, near*

Read the explanation, and study the examples. Complete the exercises that follow.

> **Explanation 3:** <u>Beside</u> and often <u>by</u> indicate that two people or things are *very* near—touching or almost touching each other. <u>Near</u> is a more general term. It does not mean that two people or things are touching or almost touching each other.

Mary sits <u>by</u> John.

Mary sits <u>beside</u> John.

Jim sits <u>near</u> John.

Mary   John   Jim

Exercise A4

Write <u>by</u> or <u>beside</u> if the two states, cities, or volumes are touching each other. Otherwise, write <u>near</u>.

1. Arizona is _____ New Mexico.

2. Chigwell is _____ London.

3. Volume A is _____ Volume B.

4. Volume C is _____ Volume A.

Two-Word Prepositions: *next to, close to, far from*

Read the explanation, and study the examples. Complete the exercises that follow.

Explanation 4: <u>Next to</u> indicates that two people or things are *very* near—touching or almost touching each other. <u>Close to</u> is a more general term. It does not mean that two people or things are touching or almost touching each other. It means they are *near* each other. <u>Far (away) from</u> and <u>close to</u> are opposites.

Mary sits <u>next to</u> John.

Jim sits <u>close to</u> John.

George sits <u>far (away) from</u> John.

George

Mary   John   Jim

 Quick Check 1

Synonyms are words that have the same meaning. For example, *talk* and *speak* are synonyms. Antonyms are words that have the opposite meaning. For example, *love* and *hate* are antonyms. Check the ones that are synonyms.

☑   1.   next to, by, beside

☑   2.   close to, near

☐   3.   close to, far from

Exercise A5

Check off the correct preposition as you write it in a blank.

☑ **next to**   ☑ **next to**   ☑ **beside**   ☑ **near**

1. Is Canada near the United States? Yes, but it's <u>more than</u> just near it; it's right
   _____beside_____ the United States.

2. Kimberly Harris doesn't live next door to me, but she does live ___near___ me in the same neighborhood.

3. Chile and Argentina share a long border. The two countries are right ___next to___ each other.

4. Volume A is always ___next to___ Volume B.

 Quick Check 2

Check the sentence if the two states are touching according to the illustration. Then write <u>next to</u> or <u>beside</u> in the blank. Write <u>near</u> in the other blanks.

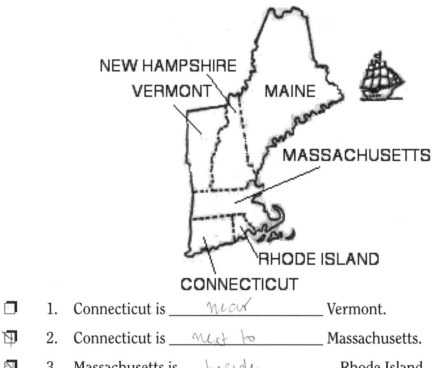

☐   1.   Connecticut is ___near___ Vermont.

☑   2.   Connecticut is ___next to___ Massachusetts.

☑   3.   Massachusetts is ___beside___ Rhode Island.

☐   4.   Vermont is ___near___ Rhode Island.

 **Quick Check 3**

Check the sentence if the two cities are touching or almost touching according to the map. Then write <u>next to</u> or <u>beside</u> in the space. Write <u>near</u> in the other blanks.

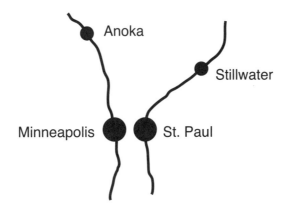

☑ 1. Minneapolis is _____ next to _____ St. Paul.

☐ 2. Anoka is _____ near _____ Minneapolis.

☐ 3. Stillwater is _____ near _____ St. Paul.

☑ 4. St. Paul is _____ beside _____ Minneapolis.

Putting It Together

Review Explanations 3 and 4. Answer the questions with complete sentences.

In your hometown or city

1. Who lives next to you?

   Amanda lives next to me

2. Who lives close to you?

   John lives close to me.

3. Who lives far from you?

   Patty lives far from me

In your class

4. Who sits next to you?

   Jeremy sits next to me

5. Who sits close to you?

   Bill sits close to me

6. Who sits far from you?

   Christine sits far from me

Quick Check 4

Check the boxes of the sentences that are INCORRECT.

☑ 1. Jose arrived in the United States <u>in</u> September 1, 1995. *on*

☐ 2. The moon is <u>far from</u> the earth.

☐ 3. England is <u>next to</u> France.

☑ 4. The President of the United States lives <u>in</u> 1600 Pennsylvania Avenue. *at*

☑ 5. I'll see you <u>on</u> 8:00! *at*

Write the incorrect sentences correctly.

_____

_____

_____

_____

Exercise A6

Choose from the prepositions listed, and fill in the blanks.

in   on   at   close to   far from

Inspector Price Solves a Murder (Part 1)

___At___ noon ___on___ May 5, 1999, the phone rang at police headquarters. The man on the
1   2

phone said that a crime had been committed ___at___ 2551 River Street. The man did not give
3

his name. Inspector John Price was assigned to the case.

When he arrived ___at___ the address, he found the body of Henry Renner lying ___in___ the
4   5

corner of his living room. He had been shot once, and a gun was also lying there ___close to___ the
6

body. Inspector Price noticed a car parked ___on___ the corner of River and Fifth. The inspector
7

learned that the car belonged to Randall Smith, a business associate of the victim.

Inspector Price Solves a Murder (Part 2)

____At____ 1:00 the same day, he drove to Randall Smith's home, which was also ____on____ River

Street not __far from__ the victim's. Smith was sitting ____in____ a lawn chair in front of his house.

Inspector Price said, "I'm afraid I have some bad news; your business associate, Henry

Renner, was found murdered ____in____ his living room this morning."

"How terrible!" cried Smith. "I visited him just last night. In fact, I have to go to his house

today to get my car. I ran out of gas last night, and I had to walk home."

"Why didn't you ask Mr. Renner to give you a ride?" asked the inspector.

"Well, my house is so __close to__ his that it was easier for me to walk."

"Are you sure there isn't another reason?"

"I didn't kill him if that's what you mean," Smith replied angrily. "Look, why don't you ask

the person who telephoned and told you about the crime? Maybe he could tell you more. I don't

even *own* a gun, so you have no reason to suspect me."

Inspector Price stepped ____by____ Smith and took his arm. "I'm afraid I do, Mr. Smith," he

said. "And now, would you please come with me?"

Question: How did the inspector know that Smith killed Renner?

_____

_____

_____

_____

PART B: Explanations 5–8

Common Preposition/Verb Combinations: *at* and *to* with *Smile, Frown, Laugh, Talk, Speak, Sing*

Read the explanation, and study the examples. Complete the exercises that follow.

> **Explanation 5:** Prepositions are often associated with certain verbs. Use <u>at</u> with <u>look</u>, <u>smile</u>, <u>frown</u>, and <u>laugh</u>. Use <u>to</u> with <u>talk</u>, <u>speak</u>, <u>whisper</u>, and <u>sing</u>.
>
> I <u>looked at</u> my book. My mother <u>smiled at</u> me. My teacher <u>frowned at</u> me. No one <u>laughed at</u> my joke.
>
> I <u>talked to</u> you on the phone. Eric <u>spoke to</u> you yesterday. Mary <u>whispered</u> a secret <u>to</u> me. The singer <u>sang to</u> us.

Exercise B1

Fill in the blanks with the correct prepositions according to Explanation 5.

1. Our teacher will look ___at___ our papers tonight and give them back tomorrow.

2. You should speak ___to___ your teacher about your grade.

3. Have you talked ___to___ John lately?

4. If you two must talk in the library, please whisper ___to___ each other.

5. Everyone laughed ___at___ the funny scenes in the movie.

Putting It Together

Review Explanation 5. Answer the questions with complete sentences. Be sure to use the correct prepositions.

You see: What happens when your mother is happy? (smile/me)

You write: <u>She smiles at me.</u>

What happens when...

1. ... you hear a funny joke? *(laugh/it)*

   <u>   I laugh at it   </u>

2. ... your father is unhappy with you? *(frown/me)*

   <u>   my father frowns at me   </u>

3. ... you want to tell your friend a secret? *(whisper/my friend)*

   <u>   I whisper to my friend.   </u>

4. ... a mother wants her baby to fall asleep? *(sing/her baby)*

   <u>   She sings to her baby.   </u>

Prepositions with Verbs Indicating Movement: *Go, Walk, Drive, Travel, Leave*

Read the explanation, and study the examples. Complete the exercises that follow.

Explanation 6: Use <u>to</u> with most verbs indicating movement from one place to another.

I <u>went to</u> school.

(traveled to, walked to, drove to, etc.)

Use <u>for</u> to indicate a destination with the verb <u>leave</u>.

I <u>left</u> my house <u>for</u> school. (School is a destination.)

<u>Or</u> I left <u>for</u> school. (School is a destination.)

my house   destination

Do not use a preposition when the verb <u>leave</u> is not followed by a destination.

I <u>left</u> my house at 8:00 (House is not a destination.)

Exercise B2

Fill in the blanks with the correct preposition according to Explanation 6. Write ø if no preposition is needed.

1. Tom Benson gets up and goes __to__ work every morning.

2. I'm tired of working. Why don't we both leave __ø__ home now?

3. I'd like to go __to__ Australia some day.

4. Columbus left __for__ the New World and arrived there 81 days later.

5. Andrew Jones left __ø__ his hometown and never went back there again.

Putting It Together

Review Explanation 6. Answer the questions with complete sentences. Be sure to use the cues in parentheses.

1. What did the astronauts do in 1969? *(go/the moon)*

   _____They went to the moon_____

2. Why isn't Carl Harris in his New York office? *(leave/California an hour ago)*

   _____he left for california an hour ago._____

3. Why can't you buy lunch? *(leave/my wallet at home)*

   _____I left wallet at home._____

Prepositions with Action and Non-Action Verbs: *Home, Downtown, Here, There*

Read the explanation, and study the examples. Complete the exercises that follow.

> **Explanation 7:** Do not use a preposition with an action verb before the word <u>home</u>.
> I want to go home. (<u>drive home</u>, <u>walk home</u>, etc.)

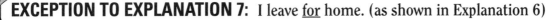

EXCEPTION TO EXPLANATION 7: I leave <u>for</u> home. (as shown in Explanation 6)

Before the word <u>home</u>, the preposition <u>at</u> is optional with some non-action verbs like <u>be</u> and <u>stay</u>:

> I am (at) home. I stay (at) home.

Do not use a preposition before the words **<u>downtown</u>, <u>here</u>,** or **<u>there</u>.**

> Let's go <u>downtown</u>.
>
> Come <u>here</u>!
>
> We'll go <u>there</u> tomorrow.

EXCEPTION: John lives <u>in</u> downtown <u>Chicago</u>. (Cities take <u>in</u>. See Explanation 9 on page 30.)

Exercise B3

Fill in the blanks with the correct preposition according to Explanation 7. Write ø if no preposition is needed.

1. Joan Bradshaw stops working and goes __ø__ home at 5:00 every day.

2. I want to go to New York City because I have never been __ø__ there before.

3. My sister has to go __ø__ downtown to pick up some things.

4. The State Capitol is __ø__ downtown.

5. How long have you been __ø__ here?

6. When are you going to be __ø / at__ home?

7. The moon is far from earth. Only 12 men have traveled __ø__ there.

Exercise B4

Reread Explanation 7, including the exceptions. Then write ø, <u>in</u>, or <u>for</u> in the space.

1. I go to work at 8:00 in the morning, and I usually leave _for_ home at 5:00 PM.

2. Larry Gray left _ø_ home and got a job when he was only 16.

3. It's fun to go _ø_ downtown and shop.

4. Many people go to the theater _in_ downtown Salt Lake City.

Putting It Together

Review Explanation 7. Answer the questions with complete sentences. Use one of these words in each sentence.

home	downtown	here	there

1. Where can you see a lot of tall buildings?

   I can see a lot of tall building downtown

2. Where are most people at 6:00 AM?

   Most people are at home at 6:00 am

3. How long was your friend in Spain last year?

   My friend was there for 1 week last year.

4. How long have you been in this city?

   I have been here for 5 years

5. Where do most people go after work?

   Most people go home after work.

Prepositions in Context

Read the following entry in Sharon Norton's diary, and answer the questions that follow using the correct prepositions. Write ø if no preposition is needed. Then read the entry again to check your work.

October 13, 2005

Dear Diary,

I had some luck on Tuesday. I got up early and talked to my roommate for a few minutes. I had some questions I wanted to ask her, but she suddenly looked at her watch and said, "I've got to leave for work or I'll be late. See you later, Sharon." She is always busy. After she had left, I wanted some breakfast. There was nothing in the refrigerator, so I decided to go to Jim's Cafe downtown. When I arrived there, I sat down at a table. In a few minutes, the waitress came, gave me a menu, and put a glass of water on the table. "I already know what I want," I told her and gave her my order. While I was waiting, I saw Marsha Elgin, a student from my math class. I called, "Marsha! Over here!" She smiled at me, came to my table, and sat in the chair next to me. When the waitress saw Marsha, she came back to the table and took her order.

"What have you been doing, Marsha?" I asked.

"Nothing much. Just studying a little for our math class. How about you?"

"The same, but I'm having problems. My roommate is a math major, but she's never home, so she can't help me. I'm really getting worried."

Marsha smiled at me again and said, "I'd be happy to help you. I'm good at math. Why don't you come over to my house tonight? We can study together."

"That would be great," I told her. "You live downtown, don't you?"

"Yes. At 657 Pendleton Street. It's not far from here—only about two blocks. Come over at seven, and we can study for a few hours."

I thanked her, and then the waitress came with our food. I was really glad I had breakfast downtown.

1. What did Sharon do first?

   She got up early _on_ Tuesday and talked _to_ her roommate for a few minutes.

2. What did Sharon's roommate do?

   She looked _at_ her watch and left _for_ work.

3. Did Sharon eat at home?

   No, she went _to_ Jim's Cafe _∅_ downtown.

4. Why?

   There wasn't any food _in_ the refrigerator.

5. What did she do at Jim's first?

   When she arrived _∅_ there, she sat at a table.

6. What did the waitress do?

   She put a glass of water _on_ the table.

7. When Sharon called to Marsha, what did Marsha do?

   She smiled _at_ Sharon and sat _in_ the chair _next to_ her. me

8. Why doesn't Sharon study with her roommate?

   Her roommate is never _∅_ home.

9. Where does Marsha live?

   She lives _∅_ downtown not _far from_ Jim's Cafe, _at_ 657 Pendleton Street.

10. When will Sharon visit Marsha?

    She'll visit her _at_ 7:00.

Two-Word Verbs and Multi-Word Verbs: *Go/Come Back, Look For, Look Up, Get Up, Put On, Take Off*

Read the explanation, and study the examples. Complete the exercises that follow.

Explanation 8: A list of common two-word verbs and their definitions follows. The 🔒 symbol means that the two-word verb is nonseparable and that no object can go between the two words. (See Beyond the Explanations on page 21.)

Two-Word Verbs	Definitions
go/come back	return
look for 🔒	search for
look up	search for and find in a book
get up	rise from bed
put on	dress in something
take off	remove a piece of clothing

Exercise B5

Fill in the blanks with the correct word according to Explanation 8.

1. I'm leaving, and I will never come ___back___ !

2. It's fun to go to the beach and look ___for___ beautiful seashells.

3. John bought Jane a bracelet. She put it ___on___ and said, "Thank you, John."

4. Could you all be quiet, please? It's 11:00, and I have to get ___up___ early tomorrow morning.

5. Al didn't know what the word meant, so he looked it ___up___ in the dictionary.

6. Before I do the dishes, I always take ___off___ my wedding ring.

Beyond the Explanations

Transitive verbs are verbs that can have an object. There are two kinds of transitive two-word verbs: *separable* and *nonseparable*. If the verb is nonseparable, no object can go between the two words of the two-word verb. That is, the object must go <u>after</u> the two-word verb. Below are examples with nonseparable two-word verbs. The object *my car keys* must go <u>after</u> the two words of the two-word verb and not between.

Nonseparable Two-Word Verb

Correct:	I looked for *my car keys.*	(The object goes after the two-word verb.)
Incorrect:	*looked <u>my car keys</u> for.*	(The object cannot go between the two words of this two-word verb.)

If the verb is separable, however, you can put the object either after <u>or</u> between the two words. In the following, *his number* is the object, and it can go after <u>or</u> between the two words of the two-word verb:

Separable Two-Word Verb

Correct:	I looked up *his number.*	(The object can go <u>after</u> the two-word verb.)
Correct:	I looked *his number* up.	(The object can also go <u>between</u> the two words of the two-word verb.)

In the explanations for two-word words, all nonseparable transitive two-word verbs appear with the symbol of a lock (🔒) to indicate that the two words are "locked" together and no object can go between them.

Some two-word verbs, of course, are not transitive, and they do not take an object.

> Example: I <u>got up</u> early this morning. (<u>Get up</u> is an intransitive verb and does not take an object.)

 Quick Check 5

Review Explanation 8 to see which of the verbs are nonseparable (🔒). Then check the sentences that are INCORRECT. The object is underlined in each sentence.

- ☐   1.   Janet Rice has to look for <u>a new job</u> because she doesn't make enough money.
- ☑   2.   I'm looking <u>an inexpensive TV</u> for but I can't find one.
- ☐   3.   Come in! Take <u>your shoes</u> off and sit down.
- ☐   4.   It's cold. I'm going to put on <u>my sweater</u>.
- ☐   5.   We gave Jim a cowboy hat and said, "Put <u>it</u> on, Jim! Put <u>it</u> on!"
- ☑   6.   Where's my book? Will someone help me look <u>it</u> for?

Now, write the incorrect sentences correctly.

_____

_____

Beyond the Explanations

If a pronoun (*it, him, her, me, you, them, us,* etc.) is used for the object of a separable two-word verb instead of a noun, it must go <u>between</u> the two words.

Examples:

Correct:	I put <u>the hat</u> on.	(noun between the two words)
Correct:	I put on <u>the hat</u>.	(noun after the two words)
Correct:	I put <u>it</u> on.	(pronoun between the two words)
Incorrect:	*I put on <u>it</u>.*	(pronoun after the two words)

✔ Quick Check 6

Check the sentences that are IN.. The pronouns are underlined.

☑ 1. What do these words mean? I'm going to look up <u>them</u> in the dictionary.

☐ 2. Where is John? I'm going to look for <u>him</u>.

☑ 3. If your shoes hurt your feet, you should take off <u>them</u>.

☐ 4. Don't wear your hat during the National Anthem. Take <u>it</u> off.

Now, write the incorrect sentences correctly.

_____

_____

Putting It Together

Review Explanation 8. Answer the questions with complete sentences. Use the cues in parentheses.

1. What do you do when you lose your keys? *(look)*

    I look for it

2. After the alarm clock rings, what do you do? *(get)*

    I get up

3. Before you can remove your socks, what must you do with your shoes? *(take)*

    I take them off

4. What do you do if you don't understand a word? *(look)*

    I look it up in the dictionary

5. After a long trip, what do you do? *(go)*

    I go home

6. If you are cold, what can you do? *(put)*

    I put my coat on

Exercise B6

Choose from the following words and fill in the blanks. If no word is needed, write ø in the blank.

at   back   far from   for   in   off   on   to   up

Monday's Luck

When Ron got ___up___ on Monday morning it was snowing. He put ___on___ his clothes and
got ready to go ___to___ work. After breakfast, he looked ___for___ his car keys but couldn't find
them. It was really getting late, so he decided to call a friend from work who lived not ___far from___
him. He couldn't remember his friend's number, so he had to look it ___up___ in the phone book.
After he dialed the number, he said, "John, thank goodness you're still ___at___ home. I can't
find my car keys. Can you give me a ride to work? Thanks a million!"

When Ron and John arrived at work, it was still snowing. They ran across the parking lot.
When they were ___in___ the building, they took their coats ___off___. When Ron took ___off___
his coat, he heard a jingling sound. "Oh, for goodness sake!" he cried. "My keys are ___in___ my
coat pocket. I'm sorry, John. I should have checked my pockets before I left ___for___ work."

"That's okay," said John. "It's no big deal. Listen, I have to work all day ___in___ Building B,
but I'll come ___back___ and drive you home ___at___ 5:00, okay?"

"That would be great," Ron answered. "Thanks a lot, John. I really appreciate this."

Exercise B7

Review Explanations 1 and 2. Write the preposition that goes with each item.

1. _on_ the bench

2. _on_ the shelf

3. _on_ the roof

4. _on_ Christmas

5. _at_ midnight

6. _in_ the book (information)

7. _at_ the dinner hour

8. _on_ New Year's Day

9. _in_ the bottle

10. _in_ the bag

11. _on_ the hill

12. _on_ Cherry Lane

13. _in_ the sink

14. a ship _on_ the ocean

15. a fish _in_ the ocean

16. _in_ the bowl

17. _on_ Hollywood Boulevard

18. _on_ Independence Day

19. _on_ Highway 66

20. _in_ the hall

EXPANSION EXERCISES FOR CHAPTER 1

Complete the following assignments to expand on what you have learned in Chapter 1.

1. Write 20 sentences. Use each of the 20 items in Exercise B7.

2. Review Explanations 3 and 4. Write sentences with the prepositions <u>beside</u>, <u>near</u>, and <u>by</u>. Then write the same sentences using the synonyms <u>next to</u> (for <u>beside</u> and <u>by</u>) and <u>close to</u> (for <u>near</u>).

3. Review Explanation 8 and the exercises that follow it. Then write one sentence for each of the two-word verbs <u>look for</u>, <u>put on</u>, and <u>take off</u>. Use a pronoun like *it, him, her,* or *them* as the object in each sentence. Be sure the pronoun in each sentence is in the correct place.

4. Write for 10 minutes or more on an event in your past, such as a vacation, a birthday, etc. Use correct prepositions to tell the day, month, year, and a clock time in your story.

5. Write for 15 minutes or more on the following topic: What I Will Do Next Saturday. Use three or more of the two-word verbs shown in Explanation 8.

COMPREHENSIVE TEST 1

Write the correct word in each space according to what you have learned. If none is needed, write ø in the space.

1. The policeman looked __at__ my driver's license.

2. My birthday is __in__ June.

3. William the Conqueror invaded England __in__ 1066.

4. I haven't seen or spoken __to__ my aunt in more than a year.

5. Frank left __for__ Santa Fe this morning and should arrive there soon.

6. Shackelton traveled __to__ the South Pole.

7. Bring lots of food on the camping trip since we'll be __ø__ any stores.

8. We have to finish this work before we go __ø__ home.

9. Can you give me a ride __ø__ downtown?

10. I was already at school when I realized I had left __ø__ my books at home.

11. In the U.S., dinner is often served __at__ 6:00.

12. Please write to me __at__ 52 East 52ⁿᵈ Street.

13. Yes, I've been to Rapid City. In fact, I was born __ø__ there.

14. Look! There are many boats floating __on__ the lake.

15. How can I look __up__ a word in a dictionary if I don't know how to spell it?

16. The Brandons don't like their car, so they're looking __for__ another.

17. The play that Donna Ellis wrote is now being performed _____in_____ Broadway.

18. The students entered the room and sat _____in_____ their chairs.

19. There is a good bookstore _____on_____ the corner of First Street and Vine.

20. As punishment, I had to stand _____in_____ the corner of the room.

21. Many people like to sleep late _____on_____ Saturday.

22. You should take _____off_____ your tie before you operate this machine.

23. Jill lives only a block from me. Her friend, Alice, also lives _____near_____ me.

24. Sally left at 3:00, and no one is sure when she will come _____back_____ .

25. When Brent's parents gave him a new watch, he put it _____on_____ immediately.

26. Let's get _____up_____ before dawn tomorrow morning and get an early start.

27. There's a hardware store _____on_____ Highland Drive.

28. Mexico is right _____next to_____ the United States.

29. It's a custom to give gifts _____on_____ Christmas.

30. Richard left Brooklyn and didn't go _____back_____ for 20 years.

ANSWERS TO EXERCISES IN CHAPTER 1

A1: 1. on 2. at 3. in 4. on 5. on 6. in

A2: 1. at 2. on 3 in 4. on 5. at or on 6. in 7. in 8. in

A3: 1. in 2. in 3. in 4. on 5. at 6. on 7. on 8. at

A4: 1. by or beside 2. near 3. by or beside 4. near

Quick Check 1: Check numbers 1 and 2. The items in number 3 are antonyms.

A5: 1. next to or beside 2. near 3. next to or beside 4. next to or beside

Quick Check 2: Check sentences 2 and 3. 1. near 2. next to or beside 3. next to or beside 4. near

Quick Check 3: Check sentences 1 and 4. 1. next to or beside 2. near 3. near 4. next to or beside

Quick Check 4: Check sentences 1, 3, 4, and 5. 1. José arrived in the United States on September 1, 1995. 3. England is near (or close to) France. 4. The President of the United States lives at 1600 Pennsylvania Avenue. 5. I'll see you at 8:00!

A6: 1. At 2. on 3. at 4. at 5. in 6. close to 7. at, on 8. At 9. on 10. far from 11. in 12. in 13. close to 14. close to

Answer to question: Inspector Price did not tell Smith that there was a phone call or that the murder weapon was a gun.

B1: 1. at 2. to 3. to 4. to 5. at

B2: 1. to 2. for 3. to 4. for 5. ø

B3: 1. ø 2. ø 3. ø 4. ø 5. ø 6. ø or at 7. ø

B4: 1. for 2. ø 3. ø 4. in

B5: 1. back 2. for 3. on 4. up 5. up 6. off

Quick Check 5: Check 2 and 6. 2. I'm looking for an inexpensive TV, but I can't find one. 6. Where's my book? Will someone help me look for it?

Quick Check 6: Check 1 and 3. Note: Number 2 is correct because look for is a nonseparable two-word verb and no object can go between the two words. 1. What do these words mean? I'm going to look them up in the dictionary. 3. If your shoes hurt your feet, you should take them off.

B6: 1. up 2. on 3. to 4. for 5. far from 6. up 7. ø or at 8. in 9. off 10. off 11. in 12. for 13. in 14. back 15. at

B7: 1. on 2. on 3. on 4. on 5. at 6. in 7. at 8. on 9. in 10. in 11. on 12. on 13. in 14. on 15. in 16. in 17. on 18. on 19. on 20. in

CHAPTER 2

Prepositions for Daily Life and the Classroom

PART C: Explanations 9–13
One-Word Prepositions: *in, at* with Cities, Counties, States, Places Smaller than a City, General Locations with Activity, Places with a Visible Line or an Edge

Read the explanation, and study the examples. Complete the exercises that follow.

Explanation 9: The prepositions <u>in</u> and <u>at</u> are sometimes used to tell about where people and things are located.

Use <u>in</u> for cities, towns, countries, or states.

I live <u>in</u> Los Angeles (Morristown, Mexico, Texas).

Use <u>at</u> for places smaller than a city or town.

I'll meet you <u>at</u> the station (<u>at</u> the airport, <u>at</u> the university).

Use <u>at</u> for people and things in a general location where an activity often is going on.

We saw Bob <u>at</u> the party (<u>at</u> the soccer game, <u>at</u> the airport, <u>at</u> the movies, <u>at</u> the university, <u>at</u> the station, <u>at</u> work, <u>at</u> school, <u>at</u> the baggage claim).

Use <u>at</u> for people and things in a certain place with a visible line or edge.

John was <u>at</u> the table* (<u>at</u> the window, <u>at</u> the chalkboard, <u>at</u> the door, <u>at</u> the counter, <u>at</u> the corner of 5th and Elm, <u>at</u> the edge of the cliff, <u>at</u> the piano).

EXCEPTIONS:

Cities <u>on</u> the border/borderline	Portal is a city <u>on the border</u> between the U.S. and Canada.
Cities <u>on</u> the coast/coastline	San Francisco is <u>on the West Coast</u>.
Words <u>on</u> the chalkboard	The teacher wrote a sentence <u>on the chalkboard</u>.
Sometimes: <u>on</u> the edge	The glass was <u>on/at</u> the edge of the table.
Often: <u>in</u> the window	I saw someone <u>in</u> the window.

*<u>Note</u>: "<u>At</u> the table" refers to people who are sitting <u>at the visible edge</u> of a table. Objects rest <u>on</u> the <u>surface</u> of a table, as explained in Explanation 2 on page 2.

Exercise C1

Fill in the blanks with the correct preposition according to Explanation 9.

1. You can pay __at__ the counter.

2. There were more than 60,000 people __at__ the football game last night.

3. When I arrived __at__ the airport, my parents were waiting for me.

4. My brother and I were born __in__ Cincinnati, Ohio.

5. The city of Nogales is more than just near the Mexico/U.S. border.

   It is located exactly __on__ the border. Part of the city is __in__ Mexico, and part is __in__ the United States.

6. The teacher is standing __at__ the chalkboard now.

7. Yesterday the teacher wrote a word __on__ the chalkboard and asked, "Is this word misspelled or not?"

8. Dinner is at 6:00 sharp. I expect all of you to be __at__ the table on time.

9. Atlantic City is located __on__ the Atlantic coast.

Quick Check 7

Check the sentences containing a place smaller than a city, and write <u>at</u> in the space. Write <u>in</u> in the spaces for all the other sentences.

☐   1.   John lives __in__ New York City.

☑   2.   Get off the train __at__ Marble Arch Station.

☑   3.   Dr. Sherwood works __at__ the University of Littletown.

☑   4.   The plane landed __at__ Sky Harbor Airport.

☐   5.   Wild kangaroos can be seen __in__ Australia and New Guinea.

Putting It Together

Review Explanation 9. Answer the questions with complete sentences.

1. Where were you born?

   _____

2. Where did your airplane land?

   _____

3. Where do you get a bachelor's degree?

   _____

4. Where can I pay?

   _____

5. Where was everyone dancing last Saturday night?

   _____

Quick Check 8

All of these sentences refer to a visible line or edge. Check the sentences that contain the exceptions discussed in Explanation 9, and write <u>on</u> in the blanks. Write <u>at</u> in all of the other blanks.

☐   1.   The teacher is standing __*at*__ the blackboard.

☑   2.   The teacher wrote a word __*on*__ the blackboard.

☐   3.   Someone is __*at*__ the door.

☑   4.   Monterey, California, is located __*on*__ the Pacific coast.

☑   5.   Badajoz is a city __*on*__ the border between Spain and Portugal.

Putting It Together

All of the people in the illustration are in places that have a visible line or edge. Complete sentences 1–5 so that they tell where each person is. Use <u>at</u> in each sentence.

1.   __The mailman Mrs wilson is__ __*at*__ the corner.

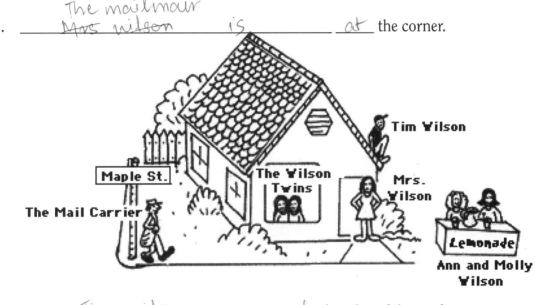

2.   __Tim wilson is__ __*at*__ the edge of the roof.

3.   __The wilson Twins are__ __*at*__ the window.

4.   __Ann and molly are at__ the lemonade stand.

5.   __Mrs. wilson is__ __*at*__ the door.

Exercise C2

Determine whether <u>at</u> indicates a *general location* or *an exact place* by writing the letter of the correct response in the blank.

1. Judson Foster lives <u>at 1515 Sawyer Road</u>.
   From this sentence you know . . .   _____ *a*
   a. the exact place where Judson Foster lives.
   b. a general location where Judson Foster lives.

2. John was injured <u>at work</u>.
   From this sentence you know . . .   _____ *a*
   a. the exact place where John was injured.
   b. a general location where John was injured.

3. Frank saw Ellen <u>at the corner of 4th and Maple</u>.
   From this sentence you know . . .   _____ *a*
   a. the exact place where Frank saw Ellen.
   b. a general location where Frank saw Ellen.

4. Frank saw Ellen <u>at the university</u>.
   From this sentence you know . . .   _____ *b*
   a. the exact place where Frank saw Ellen.
   b. a general location where Frank saw Ellen.

5. Debbie gave her money to the clerk <u>at the checkout counter</u>.
   From this sentence you know . . .   _____ *a*
   a. the exact place where Debby gave the clerk her money.
   b. a general location where Debby gave the clerk her money.

6. Chris was supposed to meet me <u>at the airport</u>, but I couldn't find him.
   From this sentence you know . . .   _____ *b*
   a. the exact place where Chris was supposed to meet me.
   b. a general location where Chris was supposed to meet me.

Common Preposition/Verb Combinations: *Be from, Come from, Arrive in, on, at,* or ø

Read the explanation, and study the examples. Complete the exercises that follow.

Explanation 10: Prepositions are often associated with certain verbs.

Use <u>from</u> with forms of <u>be</u> and <u>come</u> to indicate origin.

I'm <u>from</u> Washington State. **or** I come <u>from</u> Washington State.

Use <u>from</u> in combination with other verbs and in other contexts to indicate origin.

I walk to school <u>from</u> my house.

Kelly works <u>from</u> 9:00 AM to 5:00 PM.

My house is across the street <u>from</u> Larry's.

I can see the ocean <u>from</u> my window.

Do not use <u>to</u> with the verb <u>arrive</u>. Use <u>in</u>, <u>on</u>, <u>at</u>, or ø depending on the noun that follows.

Neil Armstrong arrived <u>in</u> the U.S. last week (<u>at</u> the airport, <u>on</u> the moon in 1969, here, downtown).

Exercise C3

Fill in the blanks with the correct preposition. If no preposition is needed, write ø.

1. It's nice to meet you. Where are you __from__?

2. The plane departed at 9:00 and should arrive __in__ Chicago at 10:00.

3. The train arrived __at__ the station three hours late.

4. I always leave home at 7:00 and arrive __at__ work at 8:00.

5. The words "Nevermore, nevermore" come __from__ a poem by Edgar Allan Poe.

6. The taxi arrived __at__ 2120 Seaside Drive.

7. The plane left for New York City and arrived __ø__ there six hours later.

8. Our mail carrier arrives __on/at__ the corner of Mountain Sky Avenue and Kenwood Lane at precisely 11:20 every day.

9. How far is it __from__ the earth to the moon?

10. The ancestors of American Indians moved __from__ Asia to the Americas over the Bering land bridge 12,000 years ago.

11. The television special was broadcast __from__ coast to coast.

12. We could not see or hear the play __from__ our seats in the back of the theater.

Common Preposition/Verb Combinations: *Listen to*

Read explanations 11 and 12, and study the examples. Complete the exercises that follow.

> **Explanation 11:** Use <u>to</u> with the verb <u>listen</u> when a noun follows.
>
> I listen <u>to</u> music while I cook dinner.

Two-Word Verbs and Multi-Word Verbs: *Pay Attention to*

> **Explanation 12:** A common multi-word verb is <u>pay attention to</u>.
>
> | Multi-Word Verb | Definition |
> | --- | --- |
> | *pay attention to* | to carefully watch or listen to someone or something |
>
> <u>Pay attention to</u> me when I am speaking.

Exercise C4

Write the correct preposition in the blank.

1. They always play music in the dentist's office, but I'm usually too nervous to listen __to__ it.

2. Please pay attention __to__ what you are doing if you use this machine.

3. The concert pianist sat __at__ the piano and began to play.

4. I studied __at__ 6:30 to midnight last night.

5. The President arrived __in__ town late this afternoon.

Putting It Together

Answer the questions in complete sentences using the correct prepositions.

1. To learn about Beethoven's music, what should you do? *(listen/it)*

   _____ I listen to it _____

2. Why does Ahmed speak such good Arabic? *(come)*

   _____ he comes from Egypt _____

3. When did you come to this city? *(arrive)*

   _____ I arrived at Cairo _____

4. To understand your teacher's directions, what must you do? *(pay attention/her)*

   _____ I pay attention to her direction _____

Exercise C5

Review Explanations 9 and 10. Then decide which preposition could logically go with each of the following:

1. _____ the fights

2. _____ the auto races

3. _____ the curb

4. _____ my doorstep

5. arrive _____ the bus station

6. _____ police headquarters

7. arrive _____ the town of Sweetwater

8. arrive _____ downtown Bombay

9. arrive _____ downtown

☑ Quick Check 9

Review Explanation 10. Then check the boxes of the sentences that are INCORRECT.

- ☐ 1. I arrived to here at 9:00.
- ☐ 2. My grandparents will arrive to Baltimore on June 4th.
- ☐ 3. The Beatles arrived to the United States in 1964.
- ☐ 4. I plan to arrive to the airport at 9:00. I'll see you there!

Now, write the incorrect sentences correctly.

_____

_____

_____

_____

Common Preposition/Verb Combinations: *Shout at/to, Yell at/to, Holler at/to*

Read the explanation, and study the examples. Complete the exercises that follow.

Explanation 13: Prepositions can change the meaning of a verb.

Use <u>at</u> to indicate a negative emotion with the verbs <u>shout</u>, <u>yell</u>, and <u>holler</u>.

The men's boss was angry and shouted (yelled, hollered) <u>at</u> them.

Use <u>to</u> to indicate a more positive emotion with the verbs <u>shout</u>, <u>yell</u>, and <u>holler</u>:

The man left without his change, so I shouted (yelled, hollered) <u>to</u> him, "Hey mister! Your change!"

Exercise C6

Write <u>at</u> if the situation indicates negative emotion. If not, write <u>to</u>.

1. The room was noisy, and the reporter politely shouted his question _____ the President.

2. When her son lost his new jacket, Dorothy Kimbly lost her temper and yelled _____ him.

3. The minister smiled and kindly shouted _____ the people in the back row, "Come up front!"

4. I have a confession to make, but please don't get angry and yell _____ me.

5. The visiting dignitaries were seated in the back, so I shouted _____ them so they could hear.

6. Patience and kind words are the best way to train your dog. It does no good to get angry and holler _____ him when he doesn't understand.

Putting It Together

1. Review Explanation 13. Think about a time when someone was angry at you and shouted. What did he or she say? Use <u>at</u> in your answer.

   The person shouted _____ me, "_____ !"

2. Review Explanation 13. Think about a similar time when someone was NOT angry at you but had to shout. What did he or she say? Use <u>to</u> in your answer.

   The person shouted _____ me, "_____ !"

Exercise C7

Choose from these prepositions, and fill in the blanks logically.

in   on   at   for   from   to

Xiangrong's First Day in the United States

When I first arrived _____ the United States, I was excited, but I was also a little nervous.
1
_____ midnight _____ September 2, 1994, my airplane landed _____ Los Angeles
2   3   4
International Airport. After I went through customs, I began to look _____ my cousin, Lee. He
5
was going to meet me _____ the baggage claim. I got my bags and waited, but Lee didn't
6
come. After about an hour, I left _____ the second floor. I knew that there was a woman
7
_____ an information counter there.
8

I told the woman _____ the counter my problem. She smiled _____ me, picked up the
9   10
phone, and spoke some words. Then she hung up the phone and asked me where I was _____.
11
I told her that I came _____ Taiwan.
12

"Is your name "Xiangrong Chen?" she asked.

I said, "Yes, how did you know?"

"They have been calling your name for more than an hour. Haven't you been paying attention
_____ the loudspeaker?"
13

I listened _____ the loudspeaker. Suddenly, I heard my name. The man using the
14
loudspeaker didn't pronounce Chinese very well, so it was difficult to recognize. Over the
loudspeaker I heard, "Xiangrong Chen, please pick up a white paging phone." I went _____ a
15
white paging phone, picked it up, and said, "This is Xiangrong Chen." Suddenly I heard my
cousin's voice. I was a little angry, so I yelled _____ him. I yelled: "Lee, where in the world
16
have you been? I've been waiting for ages!"

PART D: Explanations 14–18
One-Word Prepositions: *above, over, under, underneath, beneath, below*

Read the explanation, and study the examples. Complete the exercises that follow.

Explanation 14: Prepositions can indicate the position of one thing in relation to another. The words <u>above</u> and <u>over</u> are synonyms. <u>Under</u>, <u>beneath</u>, <u>underneath</u>, and <u>below</u> are also synonyms. These synonyms can usually be used interchangeably.

---

above   **over**

x

▨▨▨▨▨▨▨▨

y

under   **beneath**   **underneath**   **below**

The x is above (over) the shaded rectangle.

The y is under (beneath, underneath, below) the shaded rectangle.

Exercise D1

Look at the illustration. Fill in the blanks with prepositions according to Explanation 14.

1. A single star shone _____ the mountain.

2. The large plane flew _____ the smaller one.

3. The moon rose _____ the mountain.

4. The truck traveled on the road _____ the river.

5. The Green River flows _____ the bridge.

Putting It Together

1. Choose three prepositions from Explanation 14. Write three sentences that describe the location of things in the room you are in right now.

   _____

   _____

   _____

2. Draw a picture of an outdoor scene like the one in Exercise D1 on page 43. Write three sentences that describe your scene. Use a preposition from Explanation 14 in each of your sentences.

_____

_____

_____

Common Preposition/Verb Combinations: *Ask, Cost, Charge, Lend (to), Give (to), Send (to), Write (to), Buy (for), Make (for), Borrow from, Introduce to, Explain to, Repeat for, Translate for*

Read the explanation, and study the examples. Complete the exercises that follow.

Explanation 15: Verbs with both direct and indirect objects may need prepositions in accordance with sentence structures A and B. Note that sentence structure B doesn't take a preposition.

<u>Sentence Structure A:</u>

I	gave	<u>a dollar</u>	<u>to</u>	<u>my friend</u>.
		direct object	preposition	indirect object

<u>Sentence Structure B:</u>

I	gave	<u>my friend</u>		<u>a dollar</u>.
		indirect object		direct object

A or B	A only	B only
lend (to)	borrow from	ask
give (to)	introduce to	cost
send (to)	explain to	charge
write (to)	repeat for	
buy (for)	translate for	
make (for)		

Exercise D2

Fill in the blanks with the correct preposition according to Explanation 15. If no preposition is needed, write ø.

1. I wrote a letter _____ my parents last night.

2. Jane went next door to borrow a cup of sugar _____ Ann Jennings.

3. May I ask _____ you a personal question?

4. The Jones often lend their lawn mower _____ the Smiths, and the Smiths always return it promptly.

5. The children made Valentine cards _____ their parents.

6. Let me introduce you _____ a dear friend of mine.

7. Could you translate this _____ me please?

8. The teacher explained the lesson _____ the class.

9. The new highway cost _____ the taxpayers millions of dollars.

10. The mechanic charged _____ me 50 dollars.

Putting It Together

Review Explanation 15, and do the following.

1. Choose a verb from the "B only" column on page 44, and write a sentence with two objects.

_____

2. Choose a verb from the "A only" column on page 44, and write a sentence with two objects.

_____

3. Choose a verb from the "A or B" column on page 44, and write a sentence with two objects and a preposition. Then write the <u>same</u> sentence <u>without</u> a preposition.

_____

Quick Check 10

Review Explanation 15. Check the boxes of the sentences that are INCORRECT.

☐ 1. I give you my word that I'm telling the truth.

☐ 2. Could you borrow me a pen?

☐ 3. I'd like to introduce you my brother.

Now, write the incorrect sentences correctly.

_____

_____

Quick Check 11

Review Explanation 15. Check the boxes of the sentences that are INCORRECT.

☐ 1. How much are you going to charge to me?

☐ 2. This watch cost to me $27.00.

☐ 3. I want to ask you a question.

Now, write the incorrect sentences correctly.

_____

_____

Prepositions that Join Other Words to Act as Adverbs: *at all*

Read the explanation, and study the examples. Complete the exercises that follow.

Explanation 16: Use <u>at all</u> to add emphasis to a negative sentence.
Henry just sat there. He did nothing <u>at all</u>.

Exercise D3

Add emphasis to the following negative ideas by using <u>at all</u>.

1. No, I don't like this. I don't like it _____ _____!

2. John was perfectly calm. He wasn't _____ _____ excited.

3. Carol doesn't even have a dime. She has no money _____ _____.

4. No, Johnny wasn't *late* for class; he didn't come _____ _____!

Putting It Together

Review Explanation 16. Write three negative sentences in which you add emphasis by using <u>at all</u>.

1. _____

2. _____

3. _____

Prepositions in Context

Gary Martinez recorded his geology professor's lecture on tsunamis (tidal waves). When he played the tape at home, this is part of what he heard. Read the lecture, and answer the questions that follow by using the correct prepositions. Write ø if no preposition is needed. Then read the lecture again to correct your work.

Tsunamis

"Good morning. I'm sure you all are very much aware of the terrible tragedy in Asia in late 2004, and so today I'd like to introduce you to tidal waves. Let's start by calling them tsunamis, a word we borrowed from the Japanese. Most of you call these waves tidal waves, but they are not caused by tides at all. Tsunamis are usually caused by earthquakes deep beneath the surface of the sea. An underwater earthquake can cause a tsunami, and the tsunami can race over the ocean at 500 miles an hour.

"A tidal wave—a tsunami, that is—can cause incredible damage to coastal cities. But it is possible to get an early warning and to be ready before the wave arrives at our doorstep. Let me explain.

"There are many seismographs all over the world. What are seismographs? Well, they are machines that listen to the earth. They listen for earthquakes that happen under the sea. Seismographs can tell us where a tsunami is coming from and when and where it may strike land.

"The earthquake makes a shock wave, and seismographs can detect this shock wave. This shock wave travels very fast. How fast? About 60 times faster *than the* tsunami. So if it takes ten *minutes* for the shock wave to reach the seismograph station, the real tidal wave—the real tsunami—will arrive at the station in about ten *hours*. Of course, the tsunami probably isn't going to hit the station—that almost never happens. Many stations aren't on the coast. In fact, many aren't anywhere near the sea. . . ."

1.	What does the lecturer introduce?	He introduces the students _____ tidal waves or tsunamis.
2.	Are tidal waves caused by tides?	No, not _____ all.
3.	Where did we get the word *tsunami*?	We borrowed it _____ the Japanese.
4.	What are underwater earthquakes?	They are earthquakes deep _____ the surface of the sea.
5.	How fast is a tsunami?	A tsunami can race _____ the ocean at 500 miles an hour.
6.	What do seismographs do?	In effect, they listen _____ the earth.
7.	What can seismographs tell us?	They can tell us where a tsunami is coming _____ and when it will arrive _____ our doorstep, as the lecturer puts it.
8.	Will the tsunami hit the station?	Probably not. The station may not be _____ the coast or even _____ the sea.

Two-Word Verbs and Multi-Word Verbs: *Call On, Go On, Hand In, Hand Back, Tear Up, Kick Out*

Read the explanation, and study the examples. Complete the exercises that follow.

Explanation 17: The following is a list of common two-word verbs and their definitions. The 🔒 symbol means that the two-word verb is nonseparable and no object can go between the two words.

Two-Word Verbs	Definitions
call on 🔒	ask someone to answer in class
go on	continue
hand in	submit something
hand back	return something already submitted
tear up	rip to pieces
kick out	make someone leave

Exercise D4

Fill in the blanks with the correct word according to Explanation 17.

1. Harold used to be in our club. When he broke our rules, we kicked him _____.

2. The magician asked me for a ten-dollar bill. I gave it to him, and he tore it _____! Later, he gave it back to me in one piece. That was magic!

3. Vince talks too much. Yesterday he told a boring story. The story went _____ for more than an hour.

4. The teacher said, "How many of you did your homework? All of you? Great! Now, hand it _____, please."

5. The teacher said, "Yesterday's homework was very good. I will hand it _____ at the end of class."

6. The teacher said, "Please do not speak unless I call _____ you."

Putting It Together

Review Explanation 17. Answer the questions with complete sentences using the verbs from Explanation 17. Use the cues in parentheses.

1. John got a letter from his girlfriend. She said she didn't love him anymore. What did John do with the letter? *(tear)*

2. Mary and Ginny talked loudly in the theater. Some other people complained to the manager. What did the manager do? *(kick)*

3. At the beginning of class today, what did the teacher do with yesterday's homework? *(hand)*

4. At the end of class, what did the students do with their homework? *(hand)*

5. The mountain climbers got tired, but they finally reached the top of the mountain. Did the climbers stop after they got tired? *(no/go)*

6. What does your teacher do when you raise your hand in class? *(call)*

Prepositions that Join Other Words to Act as Adverbs: *for good*

Read the explanation, and study the examples. Complete the exercises that follow.

Explanation 18: Use <u>for good</u> to mean <u>forever</u> or <u>permanently</u>.

Are you ever going to come back to Brooklyn?

No, I'm leaving <u>for good</u>!

Exercise D5

Express the idea of <u>forever</u> or <u>permanently</u> by completing the following according to what you have learned in Explanation 18.

1. I always hate to go back to work after my vacations. I'd like to be on vacation _____!

2. David is homesick. After he graduates from college, he plans to go back to his hometown _____.

3. The criminal continued to break the law, so the judge had to put him in jail _____.

4. If you cheat on a test, you might get kicked out of school _____.

Putting It Together

Review Explanation 18. Write sentences with <u>for good</u> in each one.

1. quit smoking

   _____

2. go back to my old job

   _____

3. leave my home town

   _____

4. stop drinking coffee

   _____

5. stay in this city

   _____

Exercise D6

Complete the dialogue. Check off each word as you write it in the blank.

Johnny McKay Gets Kicked Out of Class

❒ **on**   ❒ **on**   ❒ **on**   ❒ **for**   ❒ **out**   ❒ **out**   ❒ **up**   ❒ **back**   ❒ **in**

Hal: You should have been in class today!

Brent: Why? Did I miss something?

Hal: You sure did. The teacher called _____ Johnny McKay, and he refused to answer her
        question. He just frowned at her.
        $\quad$₁

Brent: What did she do?

Hal: Oh, she just called _____ someone else. But later she asked everyone to hand
        _____ their homework, and Johnny wouldn't.
        ₃

Brent: Why not?

Hal: I guess he hadn't done it. Anyway, when the teacher handed _____ yesterday's
        homework, Johnny looked at his and tore it _____ !
        ₅

Brent: Wow! What did the teacher do then?

Hal: She kicked him _____ of the class for the day.
        ₆

Brent: I'm not surprised.

Hal: I wasn't either. The teacher told him that if his weird behavior went _____ any
        longer, she'd kick him _____ _____ good!
        ₈ ₉

Exercise D7

Rewrite the sentences using a pronoun (*him, her, them, it*, etc.) instead of the underlined words.

> *You see:*   I put on <u>the hat</u>.
>
> *You write:*   I put <u>it</u> on.

1. Please hand in <u>your papers</u>.

    _____

2. Don't call on <u>Johnny</u>!

    _____

3. I will hand <u>your homework</u> back tomorrow.

    _____

4. Edith tore up <u>the letter</u> after she read it.

    _____

5. The teacher kicked out <u>two students</u> when they came to class late.

    _____

EXPANSION EXERCISES FOR CHAPTER 2

Complete the following assignments to expand on what you have learned in Chapter 2.

1. Review Explanation 15, and write two sentences for each of the following: sell a car (to), read a story (to), bring flowers (to), sing a song (to), knit a sweater (for). Use Sentence Structure A and Sentence Structure B.

2. Write two or three sentences about a time when you borrowed something from someone or lent something to someone. What happened?

3. Write two or three sentences about a time when someone yelled at you. Tell why they yelled at you.

4. Write about a trip that you have taken. Include the following:

   Use the word <u>arrive</u> at least once in your story as shown in Explanation 10.

   Use the preposition <u>from</u> in the manner shown in Explanation 10.

   Use <u>at</u> to indicate a general location as shown in Explanation 9.

5. Review Explanation 17 and the exercises that follow it. Then write sentences using the words <u>call on</u>, <u>go on</u>, <u>hand in</u>, <u>hand back</u>, <u>tear up</u>, and <u>kick out</u>. If possible, use a pronoun like <u>it</u>, <u>me</u>, <u>you</u>, <u>us</u>, <u>him</u>, <u>her</u>, or <u>them</u> for the object in each sentence. Be sure the pronoun in each sentence is in the correct place.

COMPREHENSIVE TEST 2

Write the correct word in each space according to what you have learned. If none is needed, write ø in the space.

1. A hurricane is threatening the cities _____ the East Coast.

2. Could I borrow a couple of dollars _____ you?

3. Could you hold on for a minute? Someone's _____ the door.

4. Frank Boyer gets irritated at his son, but he never yells _____ him.

5. Gene introduced the past tense _____ the basic English students yesterday.

6. Hello? No, I'm sorry; Randy isn't at home. He's _____ work now.

7. How far is Bristol City, and when will we arrive _____ there?

8. I didn't want anyone to see my notes, so I tore them _____.

9. Adam doesn't listen _____ the radio in his car because it makes him nervous.

10. I got in my car, and five days later I arrived _____ downtown New York City.

11. Meredith walked barefoot feeling the cool grass _____ her feet.

12. If you misbehave in class, the teacher may kick you _____.

13. My son is back from college. He arrived _____ town just yesterday.

14. Sandra arrived _____ the university on June 5.

15. That's mine! Give it _____ me at once!

16. The flock of birds flew _____ the houses and fields and disappeared.

17. The Galleria is _____ downtown.

18. The hikers were tired, but they had to go _____ walking.

19. The Pope was far away, and the reporters politely shouted _____ him.

20. Don't put that glass of milk _____ the edge of the table; it'll fall off.

21. The Taylor family is opening a business _____ Fifth Avenue.

22. The word *algebra* comes _____ the Arabic language.

23. We enjoyed our stay here and hope that we can come _____ soon.

24. Would you like to see a trick? Okay, pick a number _____ one to ten.

25. The teacher wrote some words _____ the board.

26. Please pay attention _____ these directions; I will not repeat them.

27. At the end of class, the teacher told us to hand _____ our homework.

28. If you raise your hand, the teacher will call _____ you.

29. Matthew is tired of Chicago. He'd like to leave the city _____ good.

30. Why did this happen? We have no idea _____ all.

ANSWERS TO EXERCISES IN CHAPTER 2

C1:   1. at 2. at 3. at 4. in 5. on, in, in 6. at 7. on 8. at 9. on

Quick Check 7:   Check sentences 2, 3, and 4. 1. in 2. at 3. at 4. at 5. in

Quick Check 8:   Check sentences 2, 4, and 5. 1. at 2. on 3. at 4. on 5. on

C2:   1. a 2. b 3. a 4. b 5. a 6. b

C3:   1. from 2. in 3. at 4. at 5. from 6. at 7. ø 8. at or on 9. from 10. from 11. from 12. from or in

C4:   1. to 2. to 3. at 4. from 5. in

C5:   1. at 2. at 3. at 4. at 5. at 6. at 7. in 8. in (Bombay is a city, so <u>in</u> is correct as discussed in Explanation 9.) 9. ø

Quick Check 9:   Check sentences 1, 2, 3, and 4. 1. I arrived here at 9:00. 2. My grandparents will arrive in Baltimore on June 4th. 3. The Beatles arrived in the United States in 1964. 4. I plan to arrive at the airport at 9:00. I'll see you there!

C6:   1. to 2. at 3. to 4. at 5. to 6. at

C7:   1. in 2. At 3. on 4. at 5. for 6. at 7. for 8. at 9. at 10. at 11. from 12. from 13. to 14. to 15. to 16. at

D1:   1–4 above or over; 5 under, below, beneath, or underneath

D2:   1. to 2. from 3. ø 4. to 5. for 6. to 7. for 8. to 9. ø 10. ø

Quick Check 10: Check sentences 2 and 3. 2. Could I borrow a pen from you? or Could you lend me a pen? or Could you lend a pen to me? 3. I'd like to introduce you to my brother.

Quick Check 11: Check sentences 1 and 2. 1. How much are you going to charge me? 2. This watch cost me $27.00.

D3:   1. at all 2. at all 3. at all 4. at all

D4:   1. out 2. up 3. on 4. in 5. back 6. on

D5:   1. for good 2. for good 3. for good 4. for good

D6:   1. on 2. on 3. in 4. back 5. up 6. out 7. on 8. out 9. for

D7:   1. Please hand them in. 2. Don't call on him! 3. I will hand it back tomorrow. 4. Edith tore it up after she read it. 5. The teacher kicked them out when they came to class late. Note: The pronoun goes <u>after</u> the preposition in number 2 because <u>call on</u> is a nonseparable two-word verb and no object can go between the two words.

CHAPTER 3

Prepositions for Relating Objects to One Another and for Simple Narrating

PART E: Explanations 19–22
One-Word Prepositions: *of* to Show Possession or to Show that One Noun (or Pronoun) Is Part of Another

Read Explanations 19 and 20, and study the examples. Complete the exercises that follow.

Explanation 19: The preposition <u>of</u> can be used to show possession or to show that one noun (or pronoun) is a part of another.

To show possession:

The daughter <u>of</u> a king is a princess.

The wife <u>of</u> the President is the First Lady.

To show that one noun (or pronoun) is a part of another:

The handle <u>of</u> the door is black.

Many <u>of</u> my friends live here.

Common Preposition/Noun Combinations: *Key to, Answer to, Damage to, Injury to*

Explanation 20: Use <u>to</u> instead of <u>of</u> to show possession or to show that one noun (or pronoun) is a part of another with the words, <u>key</u>, <u>answer</u>, <u>injury</u>, and <u>damage</u>.

The <u>key to</u> mastering prepositions is patient study and frequent practice.

None of us knows all of the <u>answers to</u> life's mysteries.

An electric storm can cause <u>damage to</u> your computer.

The <u>injury to</u> the boy's arm was not serious.

Exercise E1

Review Explanations 19 and 20. Write <u>to</u> or <u>of</u> in the spaces.

1. Many _____ the states' names come from Native American languages.

2. The storm caused extensive damage _____ the cities on the coast.

3. The answer _____ your question is no.

4. Have you ever locked the keys _____ your car inside your car?

5. The children _____ the movie star inherited millions of dollars.

6. The last page _____ that book is missing.

7. Lifting carelessly can result in injury _____ the back.

Putting It Together

Review Explanations 19 and 20. Answer the questions with complete sentences using the cues in parentheses. Be sure to use a preposition.

1. Why can't you get in your office? *(key)*

   _____

2. Why didn't you raise your hand when the teacher asked a question? *(answer)*

   _____

3. What did the car mechanic do after your accident? *(repair/damage)*

   _____

4. Who is your aunt? *(sister/my mother)*

   _____

5. What is a roof? *(top/house)*

   _____

Beyond the Explanations

In English there are several alternatives to using <u>of</u>. One alternative is using <u>'s</u> instead of the preposition.

Exercise E2

Change the form of these sentences from the possessive with <u>of</u> to the possessive with <u>'s</u>.

You see: The brother of your father is your uncle.

You write: <u>Your father's brother is your uncle.</u>

1. The hands of a boxer are protected by the gloves.

   A boxer _____.

2. Who is the guardian of this child?

   Who is this child _____?

Using the preposition to form the possessive is sometimes less clear than using 's. For example, sentence 2 is much clearer than sentence 1.

    1. Who is the wife of the brother of your father?

    2. Who is your father's brother's wife?

(<u>Answer</u>: <u>Your aunt</u>)

Adjectives can provide an alternative to using the preposition <u>of</u>.

    Birds <u>of</u> America   (with a preposition)

    <u>American</u> Birds   (with an adjective)

Compound nouns in English provide a substitute for both the preposition <u>of</u> and the preposition <u>to</u>.

    1. an editor of newspapers   (with a preposition)

    2. a newspaper editor   (compound noun)

    3. the injury to his knee   (with a preposition)

    4. his knee injury   (compound noun)

<u>Note</u>: In #2 the word *newspaper* is in the singular form. It is acting as an adjective, and adjectives do not have a plural form.

Exercise E3

Change the noun phrases to compound nouns as in these examples. The compound noun will not have a preposition.

    You see: The seat of the bicycle

    You write: The <u>bicycle seat</u>

1. the keys to the car   _____

2. damage to the brain   _____

3. a pilot in the Royal Air Force   _____

4. a writer of mysteries   _____

5. a professor of mathematics   _____

Exercise E4

These phrases with prepositions are not in common use and can be considered *INCORRECT*. Rewrite them as hyphenated compound nouns. First, read the example. Notice where the hyphen (-) is placed.

Incorrect:	*a road of ten miles*
Correct:	a ten-mile road

1. *Incorrect:*   *a man of six feet*

    Correct: _____

2. *Incorrect:*   *a rock of ten tons*

    Correct: _____

3. *Incorrect:*   *a book of 350 pages*

    Correct: _____

4. *Incorrect:*   *a house of three bedrooms*

    Correct: _____

5. *Incorrect:*   *a computer screen of 15 inches*

    Correct: _____

6. *Incorrect:*   *A skyscraper of 44 stories*

    Correct: _____

One-Word Prepositions: *for* as an Exchange, as a Gift or Favor, as Purpose, as a Planned Part

Read the explanation, and study the examples. Complete the exercises that follow.

Explanation 21: Use <u>for</u> to indicate an exchange, a gift or favor, or a purpose or planned part.

As an exchange:

I paid ten dollars <u>for</u> this.

Thanks <u>for</u> the ten dollars!

As a gift or favor:

This present is <u>for</u> you! (a gift)

Would you set the table <u>for</u> me? (a favor)

As a purpose or a planned part:

What is this machine <u>for</u>? (a purpose)

I bought a radio <u>for</u> my car. (a planned part)

Exercise E5

Review Explanation 21. Write the correct preposition in the blank.

1. The mechanic said, "I'm afraid you need a new starter _____ your car."

2. A net is something used _____ catching fish.

3. When Sarah Hill was sick, her neighbor did all her shopping _____ her.

4. Is this _____ me? Thank you!

5. I traded my car _____ a motorcycle.

Exercise E6

Review Explanation 15. Rewrite the following sentences using <u>for</u>.

1. I made my daughter a toy.

   _____

2. Mr. Jones bought his son a graduation present.

   _____

3. Could you do me a favor?

   _____

Putting It Together

Review Explanation 21. Complete the assignment using what you have learned.

1. Write a sentence about something you plan to buy as a part for your house, room, apartment, or car.

   _____

2. Write a sentence about a gift you plan to buy for a particular person.

   _____

3. Write a sentence about what you did as a favor for someone.

   _____

4. Write a sentence about what you paid or gave in exchange for something.

   _____

Exercise E7

Fill in the blanks with the correct prepositions according to the explanations you have studied so far. If no preposition is needed, write ø.

A Bad Start

When I first started driving, I had an accident that cost _____ me a lot of money. It
1
happened _____ my 16th birthday just an hour after I got my driver's license. I guess I wasn't
2
paying attention _____ the road, and I ran into a parked car. There wasn't much damage
3
_____ the car that I hit—just a small scratch below the handle _____ the door. The owner
4   5
_____ the car, however, was pretty mad at me. He ran out of his house and started yelling
6
_____ me. He said he wanted a new paint job _____ his car and that I would have to pay
7   8
_____ it. To make matters worse, a police officer showed up and wrote me a ticket _____
9   10
$50.00. But that wasn't all. My father happened to be walking down the street when the accident
happened. He saw the whole thing. He came up, frowned _____ me, and put out his hand. He
11
wanted the keys _____ the car, of course, and very reluctantly, I gave them _____ him.
12   13

Common Preposition/Adjective Combinations: *Absent from, Missing from, Sick of, Tired of, Good at, Bad at*

Read the explanation, and study the examples. Complete the exercises that follow.

Explanation 22: Use <u>from</u> with the words <u>absent</u> and <u>missing</u>. Use <u>of</u> with the words <u>sick</u> and <u>tired</u>. Use <u>at</u> with the words <u>good</u> and <u>bad</u>.

How many times have you been <u>absent from</u> class?

Hey, the last page is <u>missing from</u> this book!

I'm <u>sick of</u> having the same thing for lunch every day.

Sarah is <u>tired of</u> her job. She may quit.

Gerry is very <u>good at</u> playing the guitar.

My friend Al is very <u>bad at</u> crossword puzzles.

Exercise E8

Choose a preposition and a noun to complete each sentence logically. The first one has been done as an example.

☑ **at**   ☐ **at**   ☐ **of**   ☐ **from**   ☐ **from**

☐ **gardening**   ☑ **algebra**   ☐ **swimming**   ☐ **class**   ☐ **his home**

1. You won't be able to solve this physics problem if you're bad _____*at algebra*_____.

2. If a person is good _____, other people say that he or she has a "green thumb."

3. Johnny McKay is failing geometry because he has been absent _____ almost every day of the semester.

4. I spent so much time at the beach that I actually almost got tired _____!

5. After the burglary, the police asked Mr. Tillinghass what was missing _____.

☐ **at**   ☐ **at**   ☐ **of**   ☐ **from**   ☐ **from**

☐ **housekeeping**   ☐ **sweets**   ☐ **the main gallery**   ☐ **job**   ☐ **school**

6. When the art museum opened this morning, it was discovered that two paintings were missing _____.

7. To be happy, you need to have a _____ that you like and that you're good _____.

8. The children ate so much candy that they were sick _____ for days afterward.

9. Jim's living room and kitchen are a mess as usual. He's notoriously bad _____.

10. Students who are never absent _____ tend to get better grades than those who skip class.

Putting It Together

Review Explanation 22. Answer the questions in complete sentences.

1. What task or subject are you good at?

   _____

2. What are you bad at?

   _____

3. Why wouldn't most people like to eat pizza for dinner every night?

   _____

4. Why did Janie fail Geometry?

   _____

5. How did Mr. Clement know that a thief had been in his house?

   _____

PART F: Explanations 23–26

One-Word Prepositions: *before, after, by*

Read the explanation, and study the examples. Complete the exercises that follow.

Explanation 23: The words <u>before</u>, <u>after</u>, and <u>by</u> indicate where things are located in time as illustrated below.

Use <u>before</u> to indicate a point *earlier in time than another*:

BEFORE   X

Many people brush their teeth <u>before</u> bed.

Use <u>after</u> to indicate a point *later in time than another*:

X   AFTER

You can take a vacation <u>after</u> this semester.

Use <u>by</u> to indicate a point *exactly at a time or before it, but never later.*

BY

X   X

I expect to see you all here <u>by</u> six and not a minute later.

The word <u>by</u> is also often used with a *perfect tense* (a tense with a form of <u>have</u> as the helping verb):

<u>By</u> six, I <u>had</u> already left for work.

Exercise F1

Review Explanation 23. Write the correct preposition in the blank.

1. _____ her first novel, Agatha Christie wrote many more.

2. _____ Heinrich's trip to Australia, he had never really used his English.

3. Billy Buck fell off a horse. _____ that, he was afraid to ride again.

4. I will accept your final papers until 5:00 but no later. I repeat; they must be handed in _____ 5:00.

5. The satellite will be visible only for a few seconds after midnight, so if you're not outside looking for it _____ 12:00, you'll surely miss it.

Exercise F2

When followed by nouns or noun phrases (nouns and the words that go with them), <u>before</u> and <u>after</u> are prepositions. When either is followed by a clause (a subject and a verb), it becomes a conjunction.

Review Explanation 23. Then change the underlined noun or noun phrase to a clause by writing a subject and a verb in its place. See the example. The verb is provided for you.

You see: I received a letter from Isaac before <u>his death</u>.

I received a letter from Isaac before _____.
                                                    (die)

You write: I received a letter from Isaac before _____*he died*_____.

1. Mitch changed his major three times before <u>his graduation from college</u>.

   Mitch changed his major three times before _____ college.
                                                    (graduate from)

2. Before <u>the start of a race</u>, the horses always seem nervous.

   Before _____, the horses always seem nervous.
              (start)

3. I talked to the professor after <u>the end of the class</u>.

    I talked to the professor after _____.
    (end)

4. The fishermen got up before <u>sunrise</u>.

    The fishermen got up before _____.
    (rise)

5. After <u>her speech</u> to the assembly, Amy left the building.

    After _____ to the assembly, Amy left the building.
    (speak)

Exercise F3

The word <u>by</u> is often used with a perfect tense. Write the correct perfect tense and the word <u>by</u> as shown in the example.

You see: _____ the time dinner was served, I _____ already _____
(eat)
three hamburgers, so I wasn't at all hungry.

You write: <u>By</u> the time dinner was served, I <u>had</u> already <u>eaten</u>
(eat)
three hamburgers, so I wasn't at all hungry.

1. I was late. _____ the time I arrived in class, the test _____ already _____.
    (begin)

2. The students are often quite sleepy at noon because _____ then they _____ already
    _____ in class for four hours.
    (be)

3. I'm always alert at 8:30 because _____ that time I _____ already _____
    my morning coffee.   (drink)

4. Marathon runners are exhausted at the end of a race because _____ that time, they
    _____ already _____ for a long time.
    (run)

5. A friend came to my house at 8:00 last night. I didn't mind, because _____ that time, I
    _____ already _____ dinner.
    (have)

Putting It Together

Review Explanation 23. Complete the sentences using <u>before</u> or <u>after</u>. Be sure to use the correct tense of the verb.

> *You see:* lunch/be/breakfast
>
> *You write:* <u>Lunch is after breakfast</u>.

1. occasionally authors/become famous/their deaths

    _____

2. dinosaurs/live/people

    _____

3. Native Americans/live in the Americas/Columbus

    _____

4. World War II/be/World War I

    _____

5. passengers/should arrive at the airport one hour/departure

    _____

Putting It Together

Review Explanation 23. Answer the questions with complete sentences.

Three students wanted to apply for summer school. The deadline for handing in the application was 5:00. The illustration shows when each student handed in the application.

Application Deadline for Summer School: 5:00

Sandra   Samuel   Jennifer

_____ × _____ × _____ × _____

4:00   5:00   7:00

1. What did Sandra do? _____

2. What did Samuel do? _____

3. What did Jennifer do?   _____

4. Who missed the deadline? _____

5. How many of the three people handed in the application by 5:00? _____

   Name them.   _____

One-Word Prepositions: *for, since, until*

Read the explanation, and study the examples. Complete the exercises that follow.

Explanation 24: Use <u>for</u>, <u>since</u>, and <u>until</u> to show when things take place in time. The preposition <u>for</u> can be used to show a length of time as in the illustration. However, it can also be omitted. Its use is *optional*.

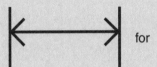

Examples:

I lived in Mexico City <u>for</u> two years.

I lived in Mexico City two years.

* *

The preposition <u>since</u> is used in a *perfect tense* to show a length of time as in the illustration.

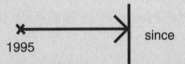

Example: I have lived here <u>since</u> 1995.

The word <u>since</u> is always followed by a point in time—not a length of time.

Incorrect: *I have lived here since <u>two years</u>.*
(length of time)

Correct: I have lived here since <u>1995</u>.
(point in time)

* *

The preposition <u>until</u> is used to show a length of time in a positive sentence as in the illustration.

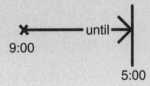

Example: I worked <u>until</u> 5:00 yesterday.

<u>Note</u>: Until may take the place of <u>to</u> in some sentences with <u>from</u>.

Correct: I worked from 9:00 <u>to</u> 5:00 yesterday.

Correct: I worked from 9:00 <u>until</u> 5:00 yesterday.

The preposition <u>until</u> is also used in negative sentences to show that something *doesn't* happen before a certain point in time as in the illustration.

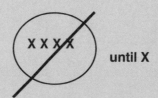

until X

Example: I'm not going to take chemistry <u>until</u> next semester.

Exercise F4

Review Explanation 24. Write the correct preposition in the space.

1. The witness said that he read _____ a few hours before going to bed.

2. I always play with my dog _____ at least an hour every day.

3. The musicians were tired at midnight because they had been performing non-stop _____ 8:00.

4. Professor Morgan has taught here _____ 1990.

5. The note on the package read, "Do not open _____ Christmas."

6. I plan to stay here _____ June 22, and then I'll have to leave because my visa expires then.

7. The dinosaurs lived from the Triassic Period _____ the end of the Cretaceous Period.

Exercise F5

When followed by noun phrases, <u>since</u> and <u>until</u> are prepositions. When either is followed by a clause (a subject and a verb), it becomes a conjunction.

Review Explanation 24. Then change the underlined noun phrase to a clause by writing a subject and a verb in its place as in the example. The verb is provided for you.

You see: I have made no friends here since <u>my arrival</u>.

I have made no friends here since _____.
(arrive)

You write: I have made no friends here since _____ I arrived _____.

1. Joe Carter went to work every morning at nine until <u>his resignation from his job</u>.

   Joe Carter went to work every morning at nine until _____ his job.
   (resign from)

2. The poor man has been in the hospital ever since <u>getting sick</u> last year.

   The poor man has been in the hospital ever since _____ last year.
   (get sick)

3. I'm not going to feel successful until <u>my graduation from college</u>.

   I'm not going to feel successful until _____ college.
   (graduate from)

4. Frederick had never known happiness until <u>his marriage to Sheila</u>.

   Frederick had never known happiness until _____ Sheila.
   (get married to)

5. The boss has changed her mind about the new project since <u>talking to her assistant</u>.

   The boss has changed her mind about the new project since _____ her assistant.
   (talk to)

 **Quick Check 12**

Review Explanation 24. Check the boxes of the sentences that are INCORRECT.

☐   1.   I'm going to get married <u>until</u> I graduate.

☐   2.   The Harris family has lived in Sri Lanka since <u>ten years</u>.

☐   3.   Mark has been working in his garden <u>since</u> 9:00 this morning.

☐   4.   The dinosaurs ruled the earth <u>for</u> 140 million years.

☐   5.   I'll be here <u>until</u> 5:30 so you can call anytime before that.

Write the incorrect sentence(s) correctly <u>without</u> changing the underlined word(s).

_____

_____

Quick Check 13

Check the boxes of the sentences that are INCORRECT.

☐   1.   I was here <u>since</u> 1991.

☐   2.   <u>By</u> the time I arrived at the party, everyone left.

Write the incorrect sentence(s) correctly <u>without</u> changing the underlined word.

_____

_____

Putting It Together

Review Explanation 24. Complete the sentences using the tense in parentheses. You will have to choose your own verb.

Part A

You see: I have _____ John since _____. (present perfect)

You write: I have <u>known</u> John since <u>1983</u>.

1. I have _____ here for _____. (present perfect)

2. I have _____ here since _____. (present perfect)

3. I _____ for _____ last night. (past tense)

Part B

Look at the timeline. It shows the future for Manuel Garcia. Write a sentence for each of the items. Use <u>until</u> in each sentence. Write a positive sentence for each item with a plus (+) sign and a negative sentence for each item with a minus (−) sign. Each sentence must be in the <u>future tense</u>.

Manuel Garcia's Future

graduate	get a job	buy a house	get married	die
X	X	X	X	X

study ——————

live in Greenville ————————————————————

work ———————————————

You see: + work/until

You write: <u>Manuel Garcia is going to work until he dies</u>.

You see: − buy/until

You write: <u>Manuel Garcia is not going to buy a house until he gets a job</u>.

1. + study/until _____

_____

2. − get a job/until _____

_____

3. − get married/until _____

_____

4. + live in Greenville/until _____

_____

Exercise F6

Study the timeline. It illustrates the life of Edgar Rice Burroughs, the author who created the character, Tarzan. Then answer the questions that follow the timeline. Refer to the numbers in parentheses for the information that you need.

Edgar Rice Burroughs

(1)	(2)	(3)	(4)	(5)
1875	1912		1850	NOW

He was born...
(Chicago)

(**He wrote** more than 90 books...)
(The most famous is *Tarzan of the Apes*, a story about an English baby in the African jungle.)

He has been dead...
(His books continue to sell.)

1912

worked at different jobs

(no success)

started writing

(He became famous very quickly.)
(His first book was *A Princess of Mars*. Readers liked it and wanted to read more of his books.)

1950

died
(Tarzana, California)
(reading the newspaper in bed)

(6)

lived

Questions

1. Where and when was Burroughs born?
2. When did he start writing?
3. How long did he write?
4. Was he famous when he died?
5. How long has he been dead?
6. How long did he live?

Short Answers

_____ Chicago _____ 1875

not _____ 1912

_____ 1912 _____ 1950

Yes, because _____ that time he had written more than 90 books.

_____ 1950

_____ 75 years

Two-Word Prepositions: *prior to, subsequent to* with Time

Read the explanation, and study the examples. Complete the exercises that follow.

> **Explanation 25:** Use <u>prior to</u> to mean <u>before</u> in expressions of time but not of place. Use <u>subsequent to</u> to mean <u>after</u> in expressions of time but not of place.
>
> The wheels of the aircraft are always lowered <u>prior to</u> landing.
>
> The hikers were very tired <u>subsequent to</u> their long walk through the desert.

Exercise F7

Review the timeline about Edgar Rice Burroughs in Exercise F6. Then complete the following using the <u>two-word</u> prepositions in Explanation 25.

1. Had Burroughs had much success _____ his career as a writer?

   No, he hadn't. Before that time, he was not particularly successful.

2. Was Burroughs famous for anything else before he wrote his first book?

   Not at all. _____ the publication of *A Princess of Mars*, he was completely unknown.

3. Did the public lose interest in Burroughs' work after he died?

   No. _____ his death, Burroughs' books continued to sell.

Putting It Together

Complete each of the following in the correct tense using <u>subsequent to</u> or <u>prior to</u>.

> *You see:*   lunch/be/breakfast
>
> *You write:*   <u>Lunch is after breakfast</u>.

1. occasionally authors/become famous/their deaths

   _____

2. dinosaurs/live/people

   _____

3. Native Americans/live in the Americas/Columbus

   _____

4. World War II/be/World War I

   _____

5. passengers/should arrive at the airport one hour/departure

   _____

Two-Word Verbs and Multi-Word Verbs: *Count On, Depend On, Put Off, Call Off, Show Up, Show Off*

Read the explanation, and study the examples. Complete the exercises that follow.

Explanation 26: The following is a list of common two-word verbs and their definitions. The 🔒 symbol means that the two-word verb is nonseparable, and no object can go between the two words.

Two-Word Verbs	Definitions
count on 🔒	depend on
depend on 🔒	count on
put off	postpone
call off	cancel
show up	arrive, appear
show off	try to get attention, act boastfully

Exercise F8

Fill in the blanks with the correct preposition according to Explanation 26.

1. We waited for Patricia for three hours, but she never showed _____.

2. There goes Billy Murphy riding his bike with no hands. He's always showing _____!

3. Because of lack of interest, the reunion has been called _____.

4. "Never put _____ for tomorrow what you can do today."

5. This magazine depends _____ freelance writers for 90 percent of its articles.

6. The whole presentation will be a disaster without you, so don't be late. We're counting _____ you!

Exercise F9

Choose from the prepositions, and fill in the blanks.

Johnny McKay Shows Up Wearing a Tuxedo

up	off	from
on	at	of

Brent: I'm glad I wasn't absent _____ the rehearsal for the play today.
                                    1

Hal: Why? What happened?

Brent: Johnny McKay showed _____ wearing a tuxedo!
                                2

Hal: You're kidding! He's playing the part _____ a cowboy. Why would a cowboy put
                                                3
_____ a tuxedo?
   4

Brent: Who knows? I guess he was just showing _____.
                                                    5

Hal: You know, Brent, this could be a real problem. Johnny has a leading role in the play.
The play could be a disaster if he goes _____ acting crazy.
                                          6

Brent: Don't count _____ it. The play has been put _____ indefinitely. Mrs. Pembrose
                        7   8
really can't depend _____ Johnny, and she doesn't think he's acting, Hal. I wouldn't
                      9
be surprised if she replaced him or even called the whole play _____.
                                                                 10

Hal: That would be a shame.

Brent: Listen, Hal. You're good _____ drama. Would you like his part?
                                     11

Hal: I don't know. Do you think Johnny would lend me his tuxedo?

Brent: Very funny, Hal.

Putting It Together

Review Explanation 26 and *paraphrase* (say or write in different words) each of the following sentences.

Example:

You see: We planned a party for Friday night, but now we're having it on Saturday night.

You write: <u>We put off Friday night's party until Saturday night</u>.

1. We planned a party but decided not to give it after all.

   _____

2. John said he'd come to the party, but I don't think he will.

   _____

3. Sarah came to class wearing a cowboy hat and playing a guitar.

   _____

4. We couldn't do our work without Fred Lawson.

   _____

Exercise F10

Write the letter of the INCORRECT part of the sentence in the blank. Then write that part the way it should be as shown in the example.

Incorrect:	Should Be:	
C	*at 5432 Spruce*	I live <u>on</u> the corner <u>of Elm</u> and Spruce <u>on 5432 Spruce</u>.
		A B C

Incorrect: Should Be:

1. _____ _____ I <u>listened to</u> a <u>radio program of two hours</u> when I <u>arrived home</u>.
                                        A   B   C

2. _____ _____ <u>The two cars mechanics</u> charged <u>us</u> $550 <u>for</u> the repair.
                                        A   B   C

3. _____ _____ <u>Subsequent to</u> departure, all passengers must get their boarding
                                        A

   passes <u>from</u> the attendant <u>at</u> the counter.
                  B   C

4. _____ _____ I <u>asked the teacher</u> to <u>explain me the exercise</u> a few minutes
                                    A   B

   <u>after</u> class.
   C

5. _____ _____ Cindy Palmer <u>is</u> going to quit <u>her job</u> until she earns enough
                                         A   B

   money <u>for</u> a car.
       C

6. _____ _____ <u>The Anderson family</u> has not traveled <u>to</u> Canada <u>for</u> 1987.
                                        A   B   C

7. _____ _____ The books <u>for</u> this course <u>cost to me</u> more <u>than $100</u>.
                                      A   B   C

8. _____ _____ I don't have the grade <u>for</u> my <u>500-word</u> composition because the
                                             A   B

   teacher <u>hasn't handed back it</u> yet.
                  C

9. _____ _____ One <u>of</u> the students complained <u>to</u> the Program Director that
                                     A   B

   his teacher never <u>called him on</u>.
                  C

10. _____ _____ <u>By</u> the time the doctor arrived <u>at</u> the hospital, the patients had
                                       A   B

   already been waiting <u>since</u> two hours.
                      C

Exercise F11

Review Explanation 20, and decide which preposition might logically go with each of the following:

1. I couldn't open my locker because I forgot the combination _____ my lock.

2. During the fierce battle, the soldier suffered a wound _____ his leg.

Review Explanation 21, and decide which preposition might logically go with the following:

3. "What _____?" means "Why?"

Review Explanation 22, and decide which preposition might logically go with the following:

4. I can't play that part. I'm terrible _____ acting.

5. Those criminals were clever _____ deception.

EXPANSION EXERCISES FOR CHAPTER 3

Complete the following assignments to expand on what you have learned in Chapter 3.

1. Review Exercise F11. Write original sentences that include the words <u>combination</u>, <u>wound</u>, <u>terrible</u>, and <u>clever</u> and the prepositions that go with each.

2. Write about something you are good or bad at doing.

3. Rewrite five of the following phrases <u>without</u> the preposition by changing the second noun to an adjective. Then write a sentence for each. The first one has been done as an example.

> *You see:* A. the jungle of Africa
>
> *You write:* <u>the African jungle</u>
>
> *You write:* <u>Tarzan grew up in the African jungle</u>.

   a. the jungle of Africa   f. the rain forest of Brazil
   b. literature of England   g. the winter in Russia
   c. farms of California   h. movies of America
   d. wine from France   i. elephants of Asia
   e. the desert of Saudi Arabia j. the pyramids of Egypt

4. Review Explanation 26 on page 85 and the exercises that follow it. Then write sentences for each of the two-word verbs in the explanation.

5. Use the information in Exercise F6 on page 78 to write a paragraph about Edgar Rice Burroughs. Try to include as much information as possible. Your *first* sentence might be: *Edgar Rice Burroughs became one of the best-selling authors in the world.* Your *last* sentence might be: *Edgar Rice Burroughs has been dead for more than 55 years, but his books are still popular today.*

COMPREHENSIVE TEST 3

Write the correct word in each space according to what you have learned. If none is needed, write ø in the space.

1. Don't say anything. I'm tired _____ hearing the same old excuses.

2. Excuse me. What is the answer _____ question number three?

3. I bought more memory _____ my computer.

4. Burroughs had finished almost 70 books _____ the time he died.

5. How many keys are there _____ this door?

6. A car's air filter traps the dirt that can cause damage _____ the engine.

7. Galveston, Texas, is _____ the Gulf Coast.

8. Could I borrow a pen _____ you?

9. I handed in my homework, but the teacher never handed it _____.

10. Five hundred dollars is missing _____ the petty cash box.

11. I lived in Louisville _____ eight years.

12. Are you here _____ the purpose of studying?

13. I'll give you $100 _____ that old book.

14. Are you good _____ repairing mechanical devices?

15. It's scary to stand _____ the edge of a cliff.

16. No one has seen Sam _____ 8:00 this morning.

17. Some people, unknown in life, have become famous _____ their death.

18. The back _____ a boat is called the stern.

19. The Smiths invited ten people for dinner, and only two showed _____.

20. The professor had to explain the concept _____ the class twice.

21. I looked the word *buckaroo* _____ in the dictionary.

22. There is an inspection station _____ the international border.

23. Vicki wants to go _____ working here for the rest of her life.

24. When shall I meet you _____ the airport?

25. _____ your final decision, you should consider everything carefully.

26. Richard danced into class on one foot. He's always showing _____.

27. Baby birds count _____ their parents for food.

28. Old John Jones plans to work _____ the day he dies.

29. Henry thinks Europe is in Canada. He's really bad _____ geography.

30. I didn't have time to clean the floor so I put it _____ until later.

ANSWERS TO EXERCISES IN CHAPTER 3

E1:   1. of 2. to 3. to 4. to 5. of 6. of 7. to

E2:   1. A boxer's hands are protected by the gloves. 2. Who is this child's guardian?

E3:   1. the car keys 2. brain damage 3. a Royal Air Force pilot 4. a mystery writer 5. a mathematics professor <u>Note</u>: In number 5, the *s* is correct in *mathematics* because *mathematics* is singular even though it ends in an *s*.

E4:   1. a six-foot man 2. a ten-ton rock 3. a 350-page book 4. a three-bedroom house 5. a 15-inch computer screen 6. a 44-story skyscraper

E5:   1. for 2. for 3. for 4. for 5. for

E6:   1. I made a toy for my daughter. 2. Mr. Jones bought a graduation present for his son. 3. Could you do a favor for me?

E7:   1. ø 2. on 3. to 4. to 5. of 6. of 7. at 8. for 9. for 10. for 11. at 12. to 13. to

E8:   2. at gardening 3. from class 4. of swimming 5. from his home 6. from the main gallery 7. job, at 8. of sweets 9. at housekeeping 10. from school

F1:   1. After 2. Before 3. After 4. by or before 5. by or before

F2:   1. he graduated from 2. a race starts or they start a race 3. the class ended 4. the sun rose 5. she spoke

F3:   1. By, had (already) begun 2. by, have (already) been 3. by, have (already) drunk 4. by, have (already) been running or have (already) run 5. by, had (already) had

F4:   1. for or ø 2. for or ø 3. since 4. since 5. until or before 6. until 7. until or to

F5:   1. he resigned from 2. he got sick 3. I graduate from 4. he got married to 5. she talked to

Quick Check 12: Check sentences 1 and 2. 1. I'm not going to get married until I graduate. 2. The Harris family has lived in Sri Lanka for ten years.

Quick Check 13: Check sentences 1 and 2. 1. I have been here since 1991. 2. By the time I arrived at the party, everyone had left.

F6:   1. in, in 2. until 3. from, until or to 4. by 5. Since 6. for or ø

F7:   1. prior to 2. Prior to 3. Subsequent to

F8:   1. up 2. off 3. off 4. off 5. on 6. on

F9:   1. from 2. up 3. of 4. on 5. off 6. on 7. on 8. off 9. on 10. off 11. at

F10:   1. B, a two-hour radio program 2. A, The two car mechanics 3. A, Prior to or Before 4. B, explain the exercise to me 5. A, isn't 6. C, since 7. B, cost me 8. C, hasn't handed it back 9. C, called on him 10. C, for or ø

F11:   1. to 2. to 3. for 4. at 5. at

CHAPTER 4

Prepositions for Describing Places and Narrating Life Events

PART G: Explanations 27–32
One-Word Prepositions: *around, along, down, through, toward(s), at, across, past, beyond*

Read the explanation, and study the examples. Complete the exercises that follow.

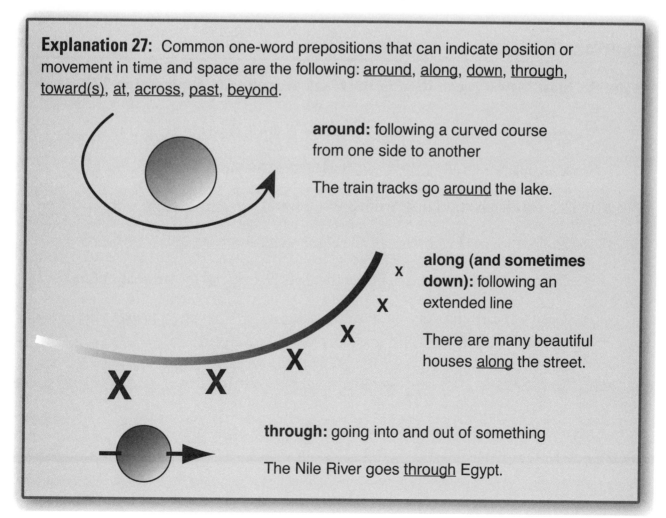

Explanation 27: Common one-word prepositions that can indicate position or movement in time and space are the following: <u>around</u>, <u>along</u>, <u>down</u>, <u>through</u>, <u>toward(s)</u>, <u>at</u>, <u>across</u>, <u>past</u>, <u>beyond</u>.

around: following a curved course from one side to another

The train tracks go <u>around</u> the lake.

along (and sometimes down): following an extended line

There are many beautiful houses <u>along</u> the street.

through: going into and out of something

The Nile River goes <u>through</u> Egypt.

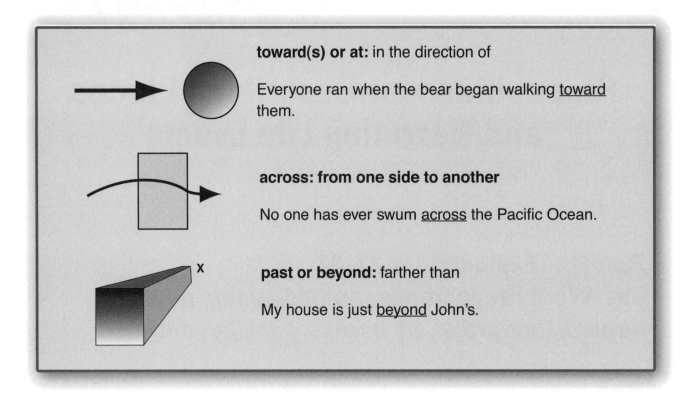

Exercise G1

Write the most logical preposition in the blank according to Explanation 27.

1. There was a large stone in the road so the cars all drove slowly _____ it.

2. There are many trees all _____ the length of the river.

3. You'll cross Eighth Street first. Tenth Street is two streets _____ it.

4. The airplane seemed to grow bigger and bigger as it flew _____ us.

5. My address is 10 Elm Street, and my brother lives just _____ the street at 11 Elm.

6. The forest was dark and scary, but I had to walk _____ it to get to the town on the other side.

Two-Word Prepositions: *away from, across from*

Read Explanations 28 and 29, and study the examples. Complete the exercises that follow.

Explanation 28: Common two-word prepositions that can indicate position or movement in time and space are <u>away from</u> and <u>across from</u>. Use <u>away from</u> to show movement in the opposite direction. Use <u>across from</u> to show that two things are facing each other.

away from: in the opposite direction

When the dog saw me, it ran <u>away from</u> me.

across from: facing

There's a post office <u>across from</u> the gas station.

Three-Word Prepositions: *catty corner from/to*

Explanation 29: A common three-word preposition that indicates position in space is <u>catty corner from (or to)</u>. It usually refers to buildings. You can also use **catty cornered from/to**, **kitty corner from/to**, and **kitty cornered from/to**.

catty corner from/to: across from diagonally

Henry and Calvin are neighbors; they live <u>catty corner from</u> each other.

Exercise G2

Check off each preposition. Write it in the correct blank.

❐ **toward(s)**   ❐ **across from**   ❐ **along**

❐ **away from**   ❐ **catty corner from**

1. The car drove slowly _____ us, disappearing in the distance.

2. Get in the cellar! There's a tornado coming _____ us!

3. The hardware store faces the bank; the two buildings are _____ each other.

4. I live on the northwest corner of Harris and Glenview, and you live on the southeast

   corner. We live _____ each other.

5. As the motorcade drove through town, the President smiled and waved to all the people

   _____ the street.

Exercise G3

Study the illustration. Write each name in the correct blank.

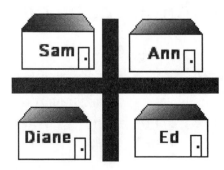

1. _____ and Ann live catty corner from each other.

2. _____ and Ed live catty corner from each other.

3. Diane lives across the street from both _____ and _____ .

4. Ed lives across the street from both _____ and _____ .

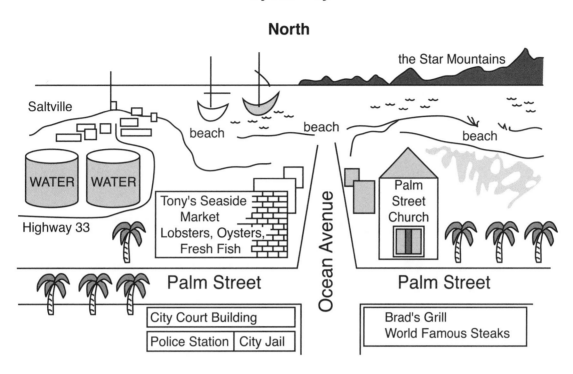

Exercise G4

Review the map of Oyster Bay. Answer the questions by writing the correct preposition in the blank. Reread Explanations 27, 28, and 29 before you begin.

1. *Question:* Where is the church in relation to Tony's Seaside Market?
   Answer: It's just _____ the street from it.

2. *Question:* Are there palm trees in Oyster Bay?
   Answer: Yes, many palms grow _____ Palm Street.

3. *Question:* Where does Ocean Avenue go?
   Answer: It goes _____ town to the beach.

4. *Question:* Are Brad's Grill and the City Court Building near each other?
   Answer: Yes, they're both on Ocean Avenue and right _____ each other.

5. *Question:* Is Highway 33 a straight road to Saltville?
   Answer: No, it goes _____ two water tanks.

6. *Question:* Is the City Court Building across the street from the church?
   Answer: Not exactly. It's _____ _____ _____ the church.

7. *Question:* If I travel north on Ocean Avenue, will I pass Tony's Seaside Market before I reach the beach?

    Answer: Yes, of course. The beach is _____ Tony's Seaside Market, and there are no buildings _____ the beach—just water.

8. *Question:* If I drive north on Ocean Avenue, where will I be going?

    Answer: You'll be going _____ the beach.

9. *Question:* What if I drive south?

    Answer: You'll be going _____ _____ the beach and out of town.

Putting It Together

Review Explanations 2, 27, 28, and 29, and study the diagram. Follow the directions to complete Parts A, B, and C.

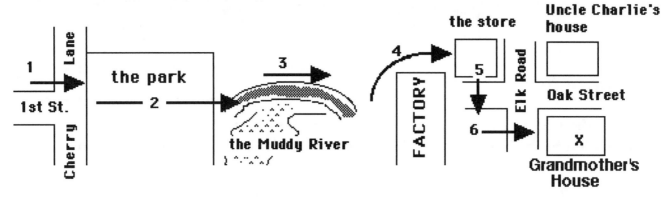

Part A

Use the words in parentheses to answer each question with a sentence.

1. Where is the store? *(catty corner from)*

    _____

2. Where is Uncle Charlie's house? *(across from)*

    _____

3. Where does Grandmother live? *(721 Oak Street)*

    _____

4. Where does Uncle Charlie live? *(the corner of Elk Road and Oak Street)*

    _____

Part B

Use the words in parentheses to answer each question with a sentence. Imagine you are standing at the corner of 1ˢᵗ Street and Cherry Lane.

1. Where is the Muddy River? *(beyond)*

   _____

2. Where is the factory? *(beyond)*

   _____

3. Where is Grandmother's house? *(past)*

   _____

Part C

Tell how to get to Grandmother's house from the corner of 1ˢᵗ Street and Cherry Lane. Use <u>through</u>, <u>over</u>, <u>around</u>, and <u>across</u>. If you wish, you may write a sentence for each of the numbers in the picture.

_____

_____

_____

_____

_____

_____

Common Preposition/Verb Combinations: *to* or *ø* with Compass Directions

Read the explanation, and study the examples. Complete the exercises that follow.

Explanation 30: Use <u>to</u> before <u>the</u> with compass directions with any verb. Otherwise, don't use a preposition.

Correct: I traveled <u>to the</u> west last year.

Correct: I traveled <u>west</u> last year.

Exercise G5

Review the map. Notice where "your house" is on the map. Then fill in the blanks according to Explanations 2 and 30. Use to, on, or ø.

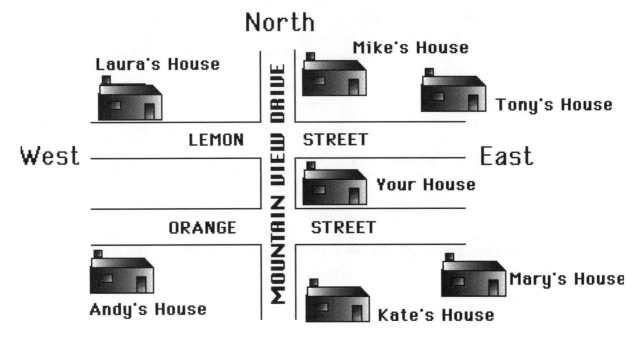

1. How do you get from your house to Tony's?

   I go _____ east _____ Lemon Street.

2. How do you get from your house to Mary's?

   I go _____ the east _____ Orange Street.

3. How do you get from your house to Mike's?

   I walk _____ north _____ Mountain View Drive.

4. How do you get from your house to Laura's?

   I walk _____ the west _____ Lemon Street.

5. How do you get from your house to Andy's?

   I go _____ west _____ Orange Street.

6. How do you get from your house to Kate's?

   I drive _____ the south _____ Mountain View Drive.

Putting It Together

Review the map of Oyster Bay in Exercise G4, and answer these questions using compass directions as explained in Explanation 30.

1. How do you get to the beach from the City Court Building?

_____

2. How do you get to Saltville from the water tanks?

_____

3. How do you get to Tony's Seaside Market from the beach?

_____

One-Word Prepositions: *in the part, on the side, at the end*

Read the explanation, and study the examples. Complete the exercises that follow.

Explanation 31: Use <u>in</u> with the word <u>part</u>, <u>on</u> with the word <u>side</u>, and <u>at</u> with the word <u>end</u>.

> <u>In</u> the northern <u>part</u> of Oyster Bay is a sandy beach.
>
> My hometown is mostly industrial, but I live <u>on</u> the south <u>side</u>, which is residential.
>
> <u>At</u> the southern <u>end</u> of Oyster Bay is the police station.

<u>On</u> is also sometimes used with the word <u>end</u> but never to describe the end of a story, a written document, a time, or an activity. Note that <u>at</u> is most always correct with the word <u>end</u>:

Correct: <u>On</u> (or at) the north end of town, there is a hill.

Incorrect: *<u>On</u> the end of the report was a list of recommendations.*

Correct: <u>At</u> the end of the report was a list of recommendations.

Incorrect: *<u>On</u> the end of the concert, everyone applauded.*

Correct: <u>At</u> the end of the concert, everyone applauded.

Incorrect: *<u>On</u> the end of the hour, class ended.*

Correct: <u>At</u> the end of the hour, class ended.

Exercise G6

Fill in the blanks according to Explanation 31.

1. Bogota is _____ the central part of Colombia.

2. If you travel to the east for six blocks, you'll see a tall building ____ the left side of the road.

3. Many people relax and watch TV ____ the end of each workday.

4. Caracas is located _____ the northern part of Venezuela.

5. The driver's seat is _____ the left side of the car in the U.S.

6. Tierra del Fuego is ____ the southern end of South America.

7. Venezuela and Colombia are ____ the northern part of South America.

8. _____ the eastern end of Silver City is a little airport.

Beyond the Explanations

In Explanation 30, you learned that with compass directions the preposition <u>to</u> is used only before <u>the</u>.

   1. Go <u>to the north</u>.   (preposition with <u>the</u> + compass direction)

   2. Go <u>north</u>.   (<u>no</u> preposition with compass direction without <u>the</u>)

Often, however, the word <u>part</u> is <u>understood</u> but not written. In this case, <u>in</u> is used in accordance with Explanation 31.

   3. Pierre lives <u>in</u> the north <u>part</u> of France.   (<u>part</u> is written)

   4. Pierre lives <u>in</u> the north of France.   (<u>part</u> is understood)

In #4, the writer is referring to a <u>part</u> of France but doesn't write the word <u>part</u>. The reader knows that the writer means <u>part</u> because of the preposition <u>in</u>.

 **Quick Check 14**

Check the sentences in which the word <u>part</u> is understood but not written.

❑   1.   <u>In the north</u> of this state, you can catch bass in Arrow Lake, and <u>in the south</u> you can catch trout in the Salmon River.

❑   2.   The northern states of the U.S. are too cold in the winter. That's why I live <u>in the South</u> of the United States.

❑   3.   Look at the map of Asia. Do you see China? What country is directly <u>to the north</u>? It's Mongolia, isn't it?

Write yes or no in the first blank. Complete the sentence by writing <u>to</u> or <u>in</u>.

4.   In #1, are Arrow Lake and the Salmon River <u>in</u> the state? _____ , they are _____ the north and south parts, respectively.

5.   In #2, is the writer's home <u>in</u> the United States? _____ , it's _____ the southern part.

6.   In #3, is Mongolia <u>in</u> a part of China? _____ , it's _____ the north. It's a different country. It isn't _____ China at all.

<u>Note</u>: The answer to #6 is, No, it's <u>to</u> the north. . . . It isn't <u>in</u> China at all. With compass directions, then, <u>in</u> is only used when one place is <u>in a part</u> of another place.

Write <u>Yes</u> or <u>No</u> in the first blank. Complete the sentence by writing <u>to</u>, ø, or <u>in</u>. Write <u>in</u> only when one place is <u>in a part</u> of another.

❑   7.   Is Canada in the United States? _____ , Canada is _____ the north.

❑   8.   Is England in France? _____ , England is _____ the north of France.

❑   9.   Is South Africa in Africa? _____ , it's _____ the south of Africa.

❑   10.   Is Texas in the United States? _____ , Texas is _____ the South.

❑   11.   Is Florida in Cuba? _____ , Florida is _____ the north of Cuba.

❑   12.   Is Korea in Japan? _____ , Korea is _____ west of Japan.

❑   13.   Is Mexico in the United States? _____ , Mexico is _____ south of the United States.

❑   14.   Is Shanghai in China? _____ , it's _____ the east.

❑   15.   Is New Delhi in India? _____ , it's _____ the north of the country.

Now check all the sentences in which <u>part</u> is understood but not written.

Exercise G7

Gabriela is from a very small country named Diamonia. It has only one university, one mountain range, one river, and one lake. This is a map of her country:

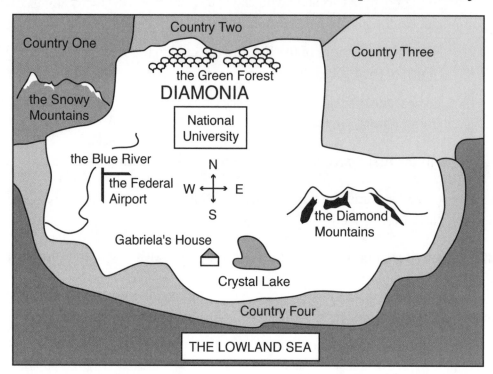

Write Yes or No in the first blank. Then complete the sentence by writing to, ø, or in. Write in when one place is in a part of another.

1. Is Country Two in Diamonia? _____ , it's _____ the north.

2. Is Country One in Diamonia? _____ , it's _____ the northwest.

3. Is the Green Forest in Diamonia? _____ , it's _____ the northern part.

4. Is the Blue River in Diamonia? _____ , it's _____ the west.

5. Is Crystal Lake in Diamonia? _____ , it's _____ the southern part.

6. Are the Snowy Mountains in Diamonia? _____ , they are _____ west of the country.

7. Is the Lowland Sea in Diamonia? _____ , it's _____ south.

Write the correct preposition and the correct place in each blank.

8. _____ the eastern part of Diamonia are _____ .

9. _____ the northern end of Diamonia is _____ .

10. _____ the northeast of Diamonia is _____ .

Putting It Together

Part A

Review the map of Diamonia, and answer these questions with complete sentences.

1. Where is Gabriela's house?

   _____

2. Where is Country Four?

   _____

3. Where is the Federal Airport?

   _____

4. Where is National University?

   _____

5. Where are the Diamond Mountains?

   _____

Part B

Review the map of Diamonia, and answer the questions with complete sentences using compass directions *(north, south, east, west)* and <u>to</u> or ø. Do not use <u>in</u>.

You see: You are at the airport. How do you get to the Diamond Mountains?

You write: <u>Go east</u>.

or

<u>Go to the east</u>.

You see: You are at the airport. Where are the Diamond Mountains?

You write: <u>They are to the east</u>.

or

<u>They are east</u>.

1. You are at the university. How do you get to the Green Forest?

   _____

2. You are in Country Two. Where is the Green Forest?

   _____

3. You are in Gabriela's house. How do you get to Crystal Lake?

   _____

4. You are swimming in Crystal Lake. Where is Gabriela's house?

   _____

5. You are in Gabriela's house. How do you get to National University?

   _____

6. You are in Country Three. Where is the Green Forest?

   _____

7. You are in Country Three. How do you get to the Diamond Mountains?

   _____

One-Word Prepositions: *by* to Indicate Manner, to Answer a *How* Question, in Passive Voice

Read the explanation, and study the examples. Complete the exercises that follow.

Explanation 32: Use <u>by</u> to indicate manner, to answer a *how* question, and to help express the passive voice.

> This vase was made <u>by</u> hand. (manner)
>
> How do people communicate?
>
> People communicate <u>by</u> speaking and writing. (the answer to a *how* question)
>
> *Antigone* was written <u>by</u> Sophocles. (passive voice)

Exercise G8

Fill in the blank with the correct preposition.

1. The airplane was invented _____ the Wright brothers.

2. I make decisions _____ carefully considering all the options.

3. The criminal was captured _____ the police.

Beyond the Explanations

To change a sentence to the passive voice, follow these steps.

Active Voice: The tornado destroyed the town.

Step 1. Write the object as the subject.	**The town**
Step 2. Write <u>be</u> with the correct number and tense.	**was**
Step 3. Write the past participle of the main verb.	**destroyed**
Step 4. Write <u>by</u> and the original subject. (often optional)	**by the tornado.**

Passive Voice: The town was destroyed by the tornado.

Exercise G9

Write the passive form of each of the following sentences according to Steps 1–4 on page 105. Use <u>by</u> in each sentence.

1. Last year's earthquake damaged the bridge to Littletown.

   _____

2. The Aztecs built many pyramids.

   _____

3. The Japanese produce automobiles.

   _____

4. Mary Brown will play the role of Juliet in the play.

   _____

5. Paleontologists in Wyoming have discovered a new dinosaur.

   _____

Putting It Together

Practice the passive voice by writing three active sentences with a subject, a verb, and an object. Change the sentences to the passive voice as in the example.

	Subject	**Verb**	**Object**
Active Voice:	**We**	**speak**	**English** **here.**
Passive Voice:	**English is spoken here.**		

1. _____

   _____

2. _____

   _____

3. _____

   _____

PART H: Explanations 33–38
One-Word Prepositions: *in, on, by* with Means of Transportation

Read the explanation, and study the examples. Complete the exercises that follow.

Explanation 33: For means of transportation, use <u>in</u> for cars and taxis and <u>on</u> for trains, ships, large airplanes, and bicycles.

> When I arrived in New York, I got <u>in</u> a <u>taxi</u> and said, "Sixty-seventh and Central Park West, please!"

> More people travel <u>in cars</u> than on planes.

> Gene came here <u>on</u> a <u>train</u> (a ship, a plane, a bicycle).

Use <u>by</u> *alone* with any singular means of transportation.

Correct: Not as many people travel <u>by ship</u> today as in the past.

Incorrect: I came here by <u>my</u> bicycle.

Correct: I came here by bicycle.

Incorrect: The mayor arrived by <u>a</u> taxi.

Correct: The mayor arrived by taxi.

Exception: on foot

When his horse ran away, the cowboy had to finish his journey <u>on foot</u>.

Exercise H1

Fill the blanks according to Explanation 33.

1. Going to school _____ a bicycle can save money.

2. Going to school _____ bicycle can save money.

3. Going to school _____ bicycles can save money.

4. I came here _____ a taxi.

5. I came here _____ taxi.

6. I came here _____ foot.

Beyond the Explanations

Notice that with <u>in</u> and <u>on</u>, the article <u>a</u> can go between the preposition and the noun. You could also put a possessive adjective (*my, your, his, her, our,* etc.) between the preposition and the noun.

Correct:	I came here in <u>a</u> car.	(article)
Correct:	I came here in <u>my</u> car.	(possessive adjective)

However, to show a means of transportation with the preposition <u>by</u>, no article or possessive adjective can be put between the preposition <u>by</u> and the following means of transportation.

Incorrect:	*Columbus came to America by <u>a</u> sailing ship.*	(article)
Correct:	Columbus came to America <u>by</u> sailing ship.	
Incorrect:	*I arrived here by <u>my</u> car.*	(possessive adjective)
Correct:	I arrived here <u>by</u> car.	

In addition, the means of transportation following <u>by</u> in such sentences cannot be plural.

Incorrect:	*Hundreds of baseball fans traveled here <u>by planes</u>.*	(plural)
Correct:	Hundreds of baseball fans traveled here <u>by plane</u>.	
Correct:	Hundreds of baseball fans traveled here <u>on planes</u>.	

 Quick Check 15

Check the sentences that are INCORRECT, according to the information in the Beyond the Explanations section and Explanation 33.

☐   1.   Many students come to school <u>by</u> bicycles.

☐   2.   Traveling by <u>a plane</u> can be fun.

☐   3.   The best way to see the country is <u>on</u> train.

☐   4.   I had to get here in <u>taxi</u>.

☐   5.   Traveling by bus is safer than traveling <u>by</u> a car.

☐   6.   Rhonda came to school <u>on</u> a bicycle.

Now write the incorrect sentences correctly WITHOUT changing the underlined word or words.

_____

_____

_____

_____

_____

Exercise H2

Write the correct preposition in the blank.

1. In this city, almost everyone travels _____ car.

2. Jack sailed _____ a ship from San Francisco to Pusan, Korea.

3. At any given time, many thousands of people are traveling _____ planes.

4. The craters of the moon were caused _____ the impact of meteors.

5. *Frankenstein* was first published _____ 1816.

6. A person's pronunciation can be improved _____ frequent repetition of words and phrases.

7. Our dishwasher is broken so we have to do all the dishes _____ hand.

8. This product is manufactured _____ the John and John Company.

9. Fred was told to take the bus, but he arrived here _____ a taxi.

10. In the 1500s the only way to travel to the New World was _____ sailing ship.

Putting It Together

Complete the following using what you have learned from Explanations 32 and 33.

Part A

Answer the following questions with complete sentences.

1. How did you get to school today?

_____

2. How will you go home from school?

_____

3. How can I improve my pronunciation?

_____

4. How can a person make money?

_____

5. How can you learn to play the piano well?

_____

Part B

Match the subjects with logical predicates (the part of a sentence with the verb). Write sentences with the correct preposition and a means of transportation. One has been done as an example for you.

Example: My Uncle Charlie goes to work by bus.

Subjects	**Predicates**	**Means of transportation**
❏ The criminals	❏ went to America	❏ a stolen car
❏ The president	❏ escaped from prison	❏ sailing ship
❏ Columbus	❏ arrived at the station	❏ plane
❏ Our mail carrier	☑ goes to work	☑ bus
☑ My uncle Charlie	❏ does his work	❏ a bicycle
❏ The businessman	❏ arrived in London	❏ the 9:00 train

_____

_____

_____

_____

Common Preposition/Verb Combinations:
Recover from, Retire from, Graduate from, Resign from

Read Explanations 34 and 35, and study the examples. Complete the exercises that follow.

Explanation 34: Use <u>from</u> with <u>recover</u>, <u>retire</u>, <u>graduate</u>, and <u>resign</u>.

recover from	(get better after an illness or injury)
retire from	(stop working for good)
graduate from	(get a degree)
resign from	(quit)

After Dr. Wentworth <u>recovered from</u> malaria, he went back to England.

Some people never want to <u>retire from</u> their jobs, no matter how old they become.

My literature professor <u>graduated from</u> Yale.

I <u>resigned from</u> my job because I was offered a better one.

Common Preposition/Adjective Combinations:
Get/Be Married to, Get/Be Divorced from,
Get/Be Acquainted with, Get/Be Familiar with

Explanation 35: Use <u>to</u> with <u>get/be married</u>, <u>from</u> with <u>get/be divorced</u>, and <u>with</u> with <u>get/be acquainted</u> and <u>get/be familiar</u>.

get/be married <u>to</u>

get/be divorced <u>from</u>

get/be acquainted <u>with</u>

get/be familiar <u>with</u>

Fran Aberts is <u>married to</u> my best friend.

A friend of mine just <u>got divorced from</u> his wife.

Are you two <u>acquainted with</u> each other? No? Well, let me introduce you!

I'm not <u>familiar with</u> Einstein's theory of relativity.

Exercise H3

Fill in the blanks according to Explanations 34 and 35.

1. Sheila Lawson is married _____ the Chief of Police.

2. Let's introduce ourselves and get acquainted _____ each other.

3. Are you familiar _____ John Steinbeck's novels?

4. I'd like to get married _____ a millionaire!

5. My grandfather graduated _____ Iowa State College.

6. When did Al get divorced _____ his first wife?

7. How long has Al been divorced _____ his second wife?

8. Because of personal reasons, I must resign _____ my job.

9. It's hard to retire _____ a job you've held for many years.

10. It takes some people a long time to recover _____ a traumatic event.

Exercise H4

Review the timeline about the life of Barbara Deacon. Answer the questions that follow by writing the correct preposition or preposition/verb combination in the blanks provided.

Barbara Deacon

1950	1951	1952	1953	1957	1987

got a job
as an accountant

got acquainted with
many patients and
learned about their needs

studied

worked as a nurse

retired from her job
and wrote her
memoirs

1951

caught valley fever/
had to go to the
hospital/resigned
from her job

1952

recovered from
her illness

1957

graduated from nursing school
got a job
got married to John Jones

1953

enrolled in nursing school

1958

got divorced from
John Jones

1. When did Barbara Deacon get a job as an accountant?

    She got the job _____ 1950.

2. How long did she work as an accountant?

    Not long; she caught valley fever and had to _____ _____ the hospital. Because of this, she had to _____ _____ her job.

3. What happened in the hospital?

    In the hospital, Barbara _____ _____ many patients.

4. Did she get over her illness?

    Yes, she _____ _____ valley fever and decided to become a nurse.

5. What happened in 1957?

    She _____ _____ nursing school and got a job.

6. Did she remain single?

    No, she ____ _____ ____ John Jones.

7. Did her marriage to him last?

    No, she ____ _____ ____ him only a year later.

8. How long did she work as a nurse?

    _____ 1987. At that time, she _____ _____ her job and began to write her memoirs.

Common Preposition/Noun Combinations: *Recovery from, Retirement from, Graduation from, Resignation from, Marriage to, Divorce from, Acquaintance with, Familiarity with*

Read the explanation, and study the examples. Complete the exercises that follow.

Explanation 36: The noun forms of the verbs and adjectives in Explanations 34 and 35 use the same prepositions.

His <u>recovery from</u> the disease was quick.

Hank was depressed after his <u>retirement from</u> his job.

I'll see you all after my <u>graduation from</u> college.

After his <u>resignation from</u> office, the politician disappeared from public view.

Fran Abert's <u>marriage to</u> my best friend was a wonderful occasion.

My friend's <u>divorce from</u> his wife was difficult for everyone.

They hired Jenny because of her <u>acquaintance with</u> the business.

I have no <u>familiarity with</u> Einstein's theory of relativity.

Exercise H5

Change the underlined clauses to noun phrases by writing a noun and a possessive adjective (or 's), as in the example. Be sure to include the correct preposition.

> *You see:* After <u>Barbara Deacon divorced John Jones</u>, she continued working as a nurse.
>
> *You write:* After <u>Barbara Deacon's divorce from John Jones</u>, she continued working as a nurse.
>
> or
>
> After <u>her divorce from John Jones</u>, she continued working as a nurse.

1. Before <u>John married Mary</u>, he was lonely.

   Before _____ he was lonely.

2. I haven't seen Brian since <u>he recovered from malaria</u>.

   I haven't seen Brian since _____.

3. As a courtesy, offices are made available to professors even after <u>they retire from the university</u>.

   As a courtesy, offices are made available to professors even after _____.

4. Debbie plans to continue living in the dormitory until <u>she graduates from the university</u>.

   Debbie plans to continue living in the dormitory until _____.

5. We hired Tom Daley because <u>he was acquainted with the business</u>.

   We hired Tom Daley because of _____.

6. Although <u>the mayor resigned from his office in scandal</u>, he plans to run for Congress next year.

   Despite _____, he plans to run for Congress next year.

Putting It Together

Paraphrase (write in different words) each of these sentences using what you have learned from Explanations 34, 35, and 36. If you wish, reread these explanations before you begin.

1. John became Mary's husband.

   _____

2. Jill quit her job and became a writer.

   _____

3. John is not married to Mary anymore.

   _____

4. Fran Filmore stopped working at the post office at age 62.

   _____

5. Dr. Gladstone finished high school in 1969.

   _____

6. Greg was sick with the flu, but he got better.

   _____

7. I don't know very much about American politics.

   _____

Beyond the Explanations

The verbs <u>marry</u> and <u>divorce</u> can be used without a preposition as shown in these simple sentence structures.

> Barbara Deacon <u>got married to</u> John Jones.
>
> or: Barbara Deacon <u>married</u> John Jones.
>
> Barbara Deacon <u>got divorced from</u> John Jones.
>
> or: Barbara Deacon <u>divorced</u> John Jones.

Exercise H6

Rewrite these sentences. Use <u>marry</u> and <u>divorce</u> instead of <u>get married to</u> and <u>get divorced from</u>.

1. It was a happy day when Kate got married to the man of her dreams.

    _____

2. It was a sad day when Henry got divorced from his wife.

    _____

Two-Word Verbs and Multi-Word Verbs: *Get Over, Leave Out, Turn On, Turn Off, Pass Away, Pass Out, Come To*

Read the explanation, and study the examples. Complete the exercises that follow.

Explanation 37: The following is a list of common two-word verbs and their definitions. The 🔒 symbol next to a two-word verb means that it is nonseparable, and no object can go between the two words.

Two-Word Verbs	Definitions
get over 🔒	recover from
leave out	omit
turn on	turn a switch to its positive position
turn off*	turn a switch to its negative position
pass away	die
pass out	faint, lose consciousness
come to	regain consciousness

*Note: When referring to lights, <u>off</u> or <u>out</u> may be used.

    Correct: Before I go to bed, I turn <u>off</u> the lights.

    Correct: Before I go to bed, I turn <u>out</u> the lights.

Exercise H7

Fill in the blanks with the correct two-word verb, according to Explanation 37.

1. I caught this cold two weeks ago and can't seem to _____ it.

2. The boxer was knocked out but _____ quickly and continued to fight.

3. If you don't want to indicate your race or religion on this form, you may _____ it _____ .

4. I'm going to start the movie now. _____ the lights!

5. It's 5:30 and time for the news. _____ the TV _____ !

6. Ann Taft isn't here today because her grandmother _____ .

7. If you breathe too rapidly, you could _____ .

Beyond the Explanations

Using the word <u>back</u> can indicate a sense of returning or doing an action again.

1. My grandmother writes to me, but I never write her <u>back</u>.

2. I lent you my pen, but you never gave it <u>back to</u> me.

3. Karen sent a letter to her cousin, but her cousin sent it <u>back to</u> her.

<u>Back</u> goes before a preposition as illustrated in sentences 2 and 3 above. In two-word verbs, <u>back</u> also goes before the particle.

1. I told Johnny to leave, and when he returned, I kicked him <u>back out</u>.

2. I turned off the radio, but my sister said, "Turn that radio <u>back on</u>!"

3. Jim handed in his homework. The teacher saw that he had not finished it, so she handed it <u>back to</u> him and told him to hand it <u>back in</u> the next day.

4. When Ruth Clawson turned off the TV, her son turned it <u>back on</u>. She immediately turned it <u>back off</u> and then unplugged it.

Exercise H8

As with other verbs, the past participle forms of transitive two-word verbs can act as adjectives. They can be called participial adjectives.

Study these examples. Complete numbers 1–4 in the same way as the examples. Write the passive sentences the way you did in Exercise G9 on page 106.

a two-word verb in an active sentence:	a two-word verb in a passive sentence:	a two-word verb as a participial adjective:
Johnny <u>tore up</u> the paper.	**The paper was <u>torn up</u>.**	**The paper lay on the floor, <u>torn up</u>.**

A two-word verb in an active sentence: **My friends left me out.**

Write the sentence above as a passive sentence.

1. I _____

Write the sentence again using the two-word verb as a participial adjective.

2. I felt _____ _____ .

Two-word verb in an active sentence: **You will turn off the TV at noon.**

Write the sentence above as a passive sentence.

3. The TV _____.

Write the sentence again using the two-word verb as a participial adjective.

4. The TV will remain _____ _____ from noon until six.

Putting It Together

Review Explanation 37. Answer the questions with complete sentences using what you have learned. Use each two-word verb in the explanation.

1. Is Sally Brown still sick with a cold? (Answer "no.")

   _____

2. Is my name on the list? (Answer "no.")

   _____

3. Why is it so hot in this room?

   _____

4. Why is Timothy Richards crying?

   _____

5. What can happen if you stand up too quickly?

   _____

6. What do you do after you lose consciousness?

   _____

7. What does someone do just before a movie starts?

   _____

Exercise H9

Choose from these prepositions to complete the dialogue.

Johnny McKay Turns Out the Lights

from   next to   on   at   out   off   over   to   away

Hal: Class was especially interesting today!

Brent: Why?

Hal: The teacher was ignoring Johnny McKay. Whenever he raised his hand, she would just call _____ someone else.
1

Brent: I can't blame her. Johnny's been acting pretty weird lately.

Hal: Well, I guess Johnny felt left _____ and got mad. You know he sits right _____ the
2   3
light switches. He just reached up and turned the lights _____ !
4

Brent: Oh, boy.

Hal: The teacher yelled _____ him, "Johnny McKay, you turn those lights back _____
5   6
immediately!" And he did.

Brent: Well?

Hal: Well, when the lights were turned back _____ , there sat Johnny wearing a set of
7
vampire's teeth!

Brent: Vampire's teeth?

Hal: Yeah, the kind some people wear _____ Halloween. You know, those terrible-looking
8
plastic teeth.

Brent: What did the teacher do?

Hal: Get this: She passed _____ !
9

Brent: No!

Hal: Yes. And when she came _____ , the first person she saw was Johnny. He was
10
holding her hand and telling her how sorry he was.

Brent: Well, that was nice of him.

Hal: Yes, but he was still wearing the *teeth,* Brent. So when she looked _____ him, she
passed _____ again!
   11
      12

Brent: Oh, no!

Hal: And it took her even longer to come _____ the second time!
                                          13

Brent: You know, Hal. I've been thinking about Johnny. He isn't such a bad guy. I heard that his
father passed _____ a couple of years ago. Maybe that's why he's acting the way he is.
            14

Hal: Don't you think he has gotten _____ it?
                                   15

Brent: Maybe not, Hal. It takes some people a lot longer than two years to recover _____
                                                                                   16
something like that.

Prepositions that Join Other Words to Act as Adverbs: *by mistake, by chance, on purpose*

Read the explanation. Complete the exercises that follow.

> **Explanation 38:** Use <u>by mistake</u> to mean accidentally, <u>by chance</u> to mean without plan, and <u>on purpose</u> to mean intentionally.

Exercise H10

Fill in the blanks with the correct prepositions according to Explanation 38.

1. I'm sorry; I didn't mean to step on your foot. I did it _____ mistake.

2. I met an old friend yesterday _____ chance.

3. This was not an accident; someone did it _____ purpose.

Putting It Together

Reread the story about Johnny McKay in Exercise H9 on page 122. Answer these questions by writing <u>Yes</u> or <u>No</u> in the first blank and completing each sentence logically according to Explanation 38.

1. Did Johnny McKay turn the lights off intentionally?

   _____ , he did that _____ _____ .

2. Did Johnny frighten the teacher with the scary teeth?

   _____ , and he did it _____ _____ .

3. Did Johnny try to make the teacher pass out?

   _____ , not at all. That happened _____ _____ .

4. The teacher passed out two times. The second time was also accidental, wasn't it?

   _____ , of course. Johnny was just showing off. Then he forgot to take out the teeth.

   He didn't make her pass out _____ _____ . It was accidental.

EXPANSION EXERCISES FOR CHAPTER 4

Complete the following assignments to expand on what you have learned in Chapter 4.

1. Map Exercise

    Part A   Draw a map of your hometown. Then write four sentences about your town by using these prepositions: <u>across from</u>, <u>catty corner from</u>, <u>along</u>, and <u>beyond</u>. You may simply use forms of the verb <u>be</u> in each sentence.

    Part B   Review Explanation 30, and write four more sentences about your map using compass directions. Use the sentence structure that follows.

    To get to (the) _____ in my hometown from my house, go _____ (compass direction) on (street name).

    Example:

    To get to the <u>Blue River Bridge</u> in my hometown from my house, go <u>west on Derby Drive</u>.

    Part C   Review Explanations 30 and 31, and write sentences with compass directions about things that are in your hometown and things that are out of your hometown. Begin with the following:

    _____ is to the north of my hometown.

    _____ is west of my hometown.

    _____ is in the southern part of my hometown.

2. Review the picture of Oyster Bay in Exercise G4 on page 95. Imagine that you spent some time there, and write a paragraph about it using prepositions from this chapter.

    • Tell what you did.

    • Tell where you went.

    • Describe the things you saw.

3. Review Explanation 37 and the exercises that follow it. Write sentences for each of the two-word verbs in the explanation.

COMPREHENSIVE TEST 4

Write the correct word in each space provided according to what you have learned. If none is needed, write ø in the space.

1. Columbus came to the New World _____ a ship called the *Santa Maria*.

2. Don't turn on 2nd Street; keep going. My street is one block _____ it.

3. All passengers should check in an hour _____ departure.

4. An explosion caused damage _____ the Apollo 13 Command Module.

5. Central Park is located right across the street _____ my house.

6. Let's go! I'm tired _____ waiting.

7. This was no accident. It was obviously done _____ purpose.

8. I got _____ my disappointment quickly and started some new projects.

9. I want to sell my car. How much should I ask _____ it?

10. Joey is an orphan; both his parents passed _____ when he was two years old.

11. Most people learn _____ doing.

12. Would you be kind enough to repeat that _____ me?

13. Jill's car wouldn't start so she had to go to work _____ foot.

14. Lenny picked up the parking ticket and tore it _____.

15. John Park has traveled extensively since his retirement _____ his job.

16. The brother _____ my boss got the promotion.

17. The conference will be held _____ downtown Chicago.

18. My neighbor sometimes comes by to borrow a cup of sugar _____ me.

19. More than 50 dollars is missing _____ the cash register. Who took it?

20. Paris is _____ the northern part of France.

21. The cookies I made didn't taste good because I left _____ the sugar.

22. The student was kicked _____ of school for cheating.

23. We live across from each other diagonally. You know, _____ each other.

24. That millionaire never graduated _____ high school.

25. We couldn't climb the high mountains so we had to go _____ them.

26. I was so shocked by the surprise that I passed _____.

27. I've had this cold for weeks. When will I get _____ it?

28. The woman who passed out came _____ and said, "I'm all right."

29. At midnight, Mary closed the book and turned _____ the lights.

30. Horace Greeley said, "Go _____ west, young man!"

ANSWERS TO EXERCISES IN CHAPTER 4

G1: 1. around 2. along, down 3. beyond or past 4. toward(s) or at 5. across 6. through

G2: 1. away from 2. toward(s) 3. across from 4. catty corner from/to 5. along, on, down

G3: 1. Diane 2. Sam 3. Ed and Sam 4. Diane and Ann

G4: 1. across 2. along, on, down 3. through 4. across from 5. around 6. catty corner from/to 7. beyond or past and beyond or past 8. toward(s) 9. away from

G5: 1. ø, on 2. to, on 3. ø, on 4. to, on 5. ø, on 6. to, on

G6: 1. in 2. on 3. at 4. in 5. on 6. at or on 7. in 8. At or On

Quick Check 14: Check sentences 1 and 2. 4. Yes, in 5. Yes, in 6. No, to, in 7. No, to 8. No, to 9. Yes, in 10. Yes, in 11. No, to 12. No, ø or to the 13. No, ø or to the 14. Yes, in 15. Yes, in; Check 9, 10, 14, and 15.

G7: 1. No, to 2. No, to 3. Yes, in 4. Yes, in 5. Yes, in 6. No, ø, or to the 7. No, ø, or to the 8. In, the Diamond Mountains 9. At or On, the Green Forest or Country Two 10. To, Country Three

G8: 1. by 2. by 3. by

G9: 1. The bridge to Littletown was damaged by last year's earthquake. 2. Many pyramids were built by the Aztecs. 3. Automobiles are produced by the Japanese. 4. The role of Juliet will be played by Mary Brown. 5. A new dinosaur has been discovered by paleontologists in Wyoming.

H1: 1. on 2. by or on a 3. on 4. in 5. by or in a 6. on

Quick Check 15: Check sentences 1, 2, 3, 4, and 5. (Number 6 is correct.) 1. Many students come to school by bicycle. 2. Traveling on a plane can be fun. 3. The best way to see the country is on a train (or on trains). 4. I had to get here by taxi (or in a taxi). 5. Traveling by bus is safer than traveling by car.

H2: 1. by 2. on 3. on 4. by 5. in 6. by 7. by 8. by 9. in 10. by or on a

H3: 1. to 2. with 3. with 4. to 5. from 6. from 7. from 8. from 9. from 10. from

H4: 1. in 2. go to, resign from 3. got acquainted with 4. recovered from or got over 5. graduated from 6. got married to 7. got divorced from 8. Until, retired from

H5:   1. Before John's (his) marriage to Mary, he was lonely. 2. I haven't seen Brian since his recovery from malaria. 3. As a courtesy, offices are made available to professors even after their retirement from the university. 4. Debbie plans to continue living in the dormitory until her graduation from the university. 5. We hired Mr. Daley because of his acquaintance with the business. 6. Despite the mayor's (his) resignation from his office in scandal, he plans to run for Congress next year.

H6:   1. It was a happy day when Kate married the man of her dreams. 2. It was a sad day when Henry divorced his wife.

H7:   1. get over 2. came to 3. leave it out 4. Turn off/out 5. Turn the TV on 6. passed away 7. pass out

H8:   1. I was left out. 2. I felt left out. 3. The TV will be turned off at noon. 4. The TV will remain turned off from noon until six.

H9:   1. on 2. out 3. next to 4. off or out 5. at 6. on 7. on 8. on 9. out 10. to 11. at 12. out 13. to 14. away 15. over 16. from

H10:   1. by 2. by 3. on

CHAPTER 5

Prepositions for Viewing the World, Narrating Trips and Vacations, and Describing Emotions

PART I: Explanations 39–43
One-Word Prepositions: *on, off* as Opposites

Read the explanation, and study the examples. Complete the exercises that follow.

Explanation 39: The prepositions <u>on</u> and <u>off</u> are often opposites.

The poster was <u>on</u> the wall, but it fell <u>off</u>.

Are your elbows <u>on</u> the table? They should be <u>off</u>!

Exercise I1

Fill in the blanks with <u>on</u> or <u>off</u>.

1. I can see because the lights are (turned) _____.

2. I can't see because the lights are (turned) _____.

3. Take your feet _____ the table at once!

4. Put _____ your shoes! You'll catch a cold if you walk around with your shoes _____.

5. I put some paper plates _____ the picnic table, but the wind blew them _____.

6. The electrician got a bad shock because he thought the power was _____ when it was really _____.

7. To stop a car, you take your foot _____ the gas and step _____ the brakes.

8. Joan Bentley put her hand _____ Johnny's shoulder, but Johnny shouted angrily, "Get your hands _____ me!"

9. The soup _____ the stove was beginning to burn, so I took it _____.

10. What are these books doing _____ the floor? Put them back _____ the shelf!

One-Word Prepositions: *in, out* as Opposites

Read the explanation, and study the examples. Complete the exercises that follow.

Explanation 40: The prepositions <u>in</u> and <u>out</u> are often opposites.

The criminal was <u>in</u> jail one day and <u>out</u> the next.

<u>Note</u>: <u>into</u> is often used instead of <u>in</u> with verbs indicating motion.

John went <u>in</u> (or <u>into</u>) the store and came <u>out</u> an hour later.

✔ Quick Check 16

Check the sentences in which the main verb indicates motion, and write <u>into</u> in the blank. Write <u>in</u> in the other blanks.

❏ 1. The soldiers marched _____ the country and conquered it.

❏ 2. Joe says Cleveland is the best city _____ the world.

❏ 3. The water of the Mississippi River flows _____ the Gulf of Mexico.

❏ 4. Waiter! There's a fly _____ my soup.

Exercise 12

Fill in the blank with <u>in</u>, <u>into</u>, or <u>out</u>.

1. Johnny walked _____ the class wearing a tuxedo, and the teacher kicked him _____.

2. I dived _____ the water, but it was so cold that I had to get ____ almost immediately.

3. When the earthquake struck, everyone in the building ran _____ _____ the street.

4. It's easier to go _____ debt than to get _____.

5. The doctor put the thermometer _____ the child's mouth, took it _____, and said, "Hmm, 98.6 degrees."

Two-Word Prepositions: *out of* Followed by a Noun

Read the explanation, and study the examples. Complete the exercises that follow.

> **Explanation 41:** When <u>out</u> is followed by a noun, <u>of</u> is often added.
>
> I haven't called because I've been <u>out of the country</u> for a few weeks.

 Quick Check 17

Check off the sentences in which a noun follows the preposition and write <u>out of</u> in the blank. Write <u>out</u> in the other blanks.

❏ 1. I moved _____ my house because it was too small for me.

❏ 2. I don't like my neighbors. I wish they would move _____.

❏ 3. Don't stay home so much. You really should get _____ more often.

❏ 4. I'd hate to be kicked _____ school.

❏ 5. The teacher said, "Suzy, take that gum _____ your mouth immediately!"

Prepositions in Context

Read the story about two pilots, and answer the questions that follow using the correct prepositions. Write ø if no preposition is needed. Then read the story again to correct your work.

The Pilot's Secret

Maggie and Cindy were pilots who owned a plane together. One day they wanted to go flying, so they went to the airport and got in their plane. Unfortunately, the plane wouldn't start because the battery was dead. Cindy said, "No problem. I'll *prop start* the plane."

Prop starting the plane means that one person stays in the plane while the other person gets out and turns the propeller (or prop) by hand. This can be dangerous. If the engine starts suddenly, the propeller could spin and injure the person outside. The person who turns the prop must be ready before the engine starts. He or she must rely on the person in the plane to keep the electrical switch off until they are ready. If the switch is off, the engine cannot start unexpectedly.

Cindy got out of the plane and shouted, "Is the switch off?"

Maggie replied, "The switch is off!" to assure Cindy that the electricity was not on and that it was safe to begin turning the propeller.

Cindy put her hands on the propeller and began turning it. When the propeller was in the right position, she took her hands off it. Then she shouted, "I'm ready! Turn the switch ON!"

Maggie reached for the switch to turn it on—but to her surprise and horror she found that it was ALREADY on! "Oh, my gosh," she thought. "I made a mistake! I never really *looked* at the switch. I told Cindy that the switch was off, but it was *on*! Cindy was counting on me, and I put her in danger. Thank goodness the engine didn't start before she was ready!"

Maggie looked out of the plane at Cindy. Then she called, "Switch ON!"

Cindy smiled at her and quickly turned the prop. The engine started with a roar, and Cindy got back into the plane.

"Well," she said. "Let's go flying!"

Maggie never told Cindy what had happened. She kept it a secret.

1. What did Maggie and Cindy do first?

    They got _____ their plane, but it wouldn't start.

2. How many people does it take to *prop start* a plane?

    Two. One stays _____ the plane and the other gets _____ and turns the prop (or propeller).

3. How is the propeller turned?

    _____ hand.

4. Is this safe?

    Yes, if the switch is _____.

5. Whom does the person outside the plane have to trust?

    The person outside the plane must count _____ the person inside.

6. Was the switch off when Cindy first touched the propeller?

    No. The switch had accidentally been left _____ when she first put her hands _____ the propeller.

7. Why did Maggie give incorrect information to Cindy?

    Maggie hadn't really looked ____ the switch when she replied, "The switch is _____!"

8. After Cindy moved the propeller into the right position, what did she do?

    She took her hands _____ it.

9. Did the plane finally start?

    Yes, Maggie looked _____ _____ the plane and Cindy smiled _____ her and *prop started* the plane.

10. What did Cindy do next?

    She got back _____ the plane and said, "Let's go flying!"

Putting It Together

All of these sentences are incorrect. Correct each sentence using what you have learned in Explanations 39, 40, and 41.

1. The Amazon River flows <u>into</u> Brazil and <u>out of</u> the Atlantic Ocean.

   _____

2. The porpoise jumped <u>into</u> the water, took a breath of air, and jumped back <u>out</u>.

   _____

3. When the earthquake struck, many of the museum's paintings fell <u>off</u> the floor, and we had to put them back <u>off</u> the wall.

   _____

4. It's dark. Why are the lights <u>on</u>? Could you turn them back <u>off</u>?

   _____

5. Mr. Kale can't answer his business phone because he's <u>in</u> the office.

   _____

Two-Word Verbs and Multi-Word Verbs:
Look Forward to, Look Back on, Take Advantage of, Get along (with)

Read the explanation, and study the examples. Complete the exercises that follow.

Explanation 42: The following is a list of common multi-word verbs and their definitions. The 🔒 symbol means that the multi-word verb is nonseparable and no object can go between any of the words of the multi-word verb.

Multi-Word Verbs	Definitions
look forward to 🔒	wait for the future with happy anticipation
look back on 🔒	think about something in the past
take advantage of 🔒	make good use of/benefit from
get along (with) 🔒	to have a compatible relationship (with)

Exercise 13

Fill in the blanks with the correct multi-word verb according to Explanation 42.

1. This is an opportunity that you should _____ now.

2. The two boys always argue. They don't _____ each other.

3. That was a great vacation. We often _____ it with pleasure.

4. You're going to the dentist? That's nothing to _____.

5. I have a new roommate, but we don't _____.

6. It's disappointing when you _____ something that gets called off.

7. Things are hard now, but ten years from now we'll _____ _____ these days and laugh.

8. This may be your only chance to get a job this year. I suggest that you _____ the situation.

Beyond the Explanations

The 🔒 symbol in Explanation 42 indicates that an object cannot go between any of the words of the multi-word verb.

> Correct: I look forward to <u>the party</u>.
>
> *Incorrect: I look forward <u>the party</u> to.*
>
> *Incorrect: I look <u>the party</u> forward to.*

It is, however, possible to put an *adverb* between the second and third words of some multi-word verbs.

> Correct: Shelly looks back on her summers in Vermont <u>joyfully</u>.
>
> Correct: Shelly looks back <u>joyfully</u> on her summers in Vermont.

Exercise 14

Complete the following by writing the adverb (<u>greatly</u>, <u>happily</u>, and <u>wonderfully</u>) between the second and third words of the multi-word verb. Use present tense.

1. I _____ seeing you.
   look forward to/greatly

2. My brother and I _____ our childhoods.
   look back on/happily

3. The two sisters _____ one another.
   get along with/wonderfully

Putting It Together

Paraphrase (write in different words) each of these sentences using what you have learned from Explanation 42.

1. I can't wait to see you!

   _____

2. Brad's roommate has a car, and Brad borrows it every day.

   _____

3. My boss and I work well with each other because we never argue or disagree.
   ₁

   _____

4. The memory of my days in college makes me happy.

   _____

Exercise 15

Check the prepositions as you write them in the blanks to complete the dialogue. The first one has been done as an example.

Johnny McKay Starts Getting Along

☑ **to**   ☐ **to**   ☐ **for**   ☐ **off**   ☐ **in**   ☐ **in**   ☐ **into**

☐ **out**   ☐ **up**   ☐ **of**   ☐ **on**   ☐ **on**   ☐ **on**   ☐ **along**

Brent: I'm really looking forward _____*to*_____ the play.
                                                    ₁

Hal: What play? Hasn't it been called _____ because of Johnny McKay?
                                                            ₂

Brent: No, after that little incident _____ class last week, Johnny has been acting like a
perfect gentleman. He walked _____ the principal's office and said he'd rather stay
                    3   4
_____ school than get kicked _____. And guess what? His teachers all agreed to
    5   6
give him another chance. I really think he wants to take advantage _____ the
                                                                      7
situation.

Hal: Well, I think it's a mistake. I don't want to be unkind, but who knows what Johnny
might do? He may not even show _____ for the play. I predict a disaster!
                                   8

Brent: Well, I'm not worried about it. Ten years from now we're all going to look back
_____ the play with a lot of pleasure. Count _____ it!
    9   10

Hal: Oh, you'll look back _____ it all right!
                              11

Brent: Don't be so cynical, Hal. Johnny has been getting _____ with his teachers and
                                                            12
classmates. And he has a lot of talent. Have you listened _____ him play the rhythm
                                                            13
guitar? I have. In fact, he and I are forming a little rock band together.

Hal: What? You and Johnny McKay? In a rock band? Together? Oh, man, you're really
looking _____ trouble, aren't you?
          14

One-Word Prepositions: *on* with Vacation, Trip, Picnic, and Break

Read the explanation, and study the examples. Complete the exercises that follow.

> **Explanation 43:** Use <u>on</u> for breaks, trips, vacations, and picnics.
>
> Most of the workers go <u>on</u> (a) break every two hours.
>
> Have you ever gone <u>on</u> a trip to the South Seas?
>
> High school teachers often go <u>on</u> (a) vacation in the summer.
>
> If it doesn't rain, we'll go <u>on</u> a picnic.

Exercise 16

Write <u>on</u> and the logical noun (*break, trip,* etc.) from Explanation 43. The first one has been done as an example.

1. None of the office workers is here because they are all _____*on*_____ a lunch _____*break*_____.

2. When you go _____ a _____ it always seems that a million ants show up to eat the food.

3. The astronauts went _____ a _____ to the moon.

4. I'm going _____, and I'm spending it at home!

5. Harriet's boss was angry at her because she went _____ a coffee _____ and didn't come back for more than an hour.

Putting It Together

Tell *when* you do these things. Use what you have learned from Explanation 43.

1. talk to co-workers _____

2. see new sights _____

3. forget about your job _____

4. eat in the country _____

5. get tired of driving _____

PART J: Explanations 44–48
Two-Word Verbs and Multi-Word Verbs: *Have to Do with*

Read the explanation, and study the examples. Complete the exercises that follow.

Explanation 44: The following is a common multi-word verb and its definition.

Multi-Word Verb:	Definition:
have to do with	to be about, to be related to, to regard

Cooking <u>has</u> nothing <u>to do with</u> car repair.

Exercise J1

Write <u>with</u> in each blank. Then check the logical noun or noun phrase from the following list and write it in the blank. The first one has been done as an example.

☑ **literature**   ☐ **the crime**   ☐ **mathematics**   ☐ **your radio**

☐ **rocks and minerals**   ☐ **prehistoric people**

1. Plumbing has nothing to do _____*with literature*_____ .

2. In the middle of math class, the teacher told a story about his dog. One of the students asked, "What does this have to do _____?"

3. Geology has to do _____.

4. Archaeology has to do _____.

5. I was totally innocent. I had nothing to do _____ at all.

6. There has been a complaint, and it has to do _____. You'll have to turn it off immediately.

Putting It Together

Tell what each of the following has to do with.

You see: history

You write: <u>History has to do with the past</u>.

1. botany   _____

2. biology   _____

3. psychology   _____

4. mathematics   _____

5. geology   _____

Common Preposition/Verb Combinations: *Be on, Be about, Talk about, Worry about, Think about*

Read the explanation, and study the examples. Complete the exercises that follow.

Explanation 45: Use <u>on</u> or <u>about</u> with <u>be</u>, and use <u>about</u> with <u>talk</u>, <u>worry</u>, and <u>think</u> to mean <u>regarding</u> or <u>having to do with</u>:

be on

be about

talk about

worry about

think about

<u>Note</u>: The verb <u>be</u> (is, are, was, were, etc.) may be omitted when an adjective clause is shortened to become an adjective phrase:

Correct: He wrote a story <u>that was about life in the Midwest</u>.

Correct: He wrote a story <u>about life in the Midwest</u>.

<u>Note</u>: The preposition <u>on</u> usually has a much more formal meaning than <u>about</u>:

Incorrect: She told me a wonderful story <u>on</u> Cancun, Mexico. (<u>On</u> is too formal in this sentence because stories are usually informal.)

Correct: She told me a wonderful story <u>about</u> Cancun, Mexico.
We can talk about books either formally *or* informally:

Correct: She wrote a wonderful book <u>about</u> Cancun, Mexico. (More informal)

Correct: She wrote a wonderful book <u>on</u> Cancun, Mexico. (More formal)

Exercise J2

Fill in the blanks with <u>on</u> or <u>about</u> according to Explanation 45.

1. Timothy is quite late, and his wife is worrying _____ him.

2. My English teacher speaks too fast. I never know what he's talking _____.

3. When I look back on my youth, I try to think _____ the good things and not the bad.

4. Dr. Filroy wrote a paper (that was) _____ physics, and it won her an award.

5. The title of the book is *Strange Fruit,* but that doesn't really tell me what it's _____.

Putting It Together

Rewrite the sentences using <u>on</u> or <u>about</u> as explained in Explanation 45.

1. The Beatles wrote many love songs.

   _____

2. My cousin told me a ghost story.

   _____

3. Dr. Phillips wrote an oceanography text.

   _____

4. Parents are always worried that their children aren't safe.

   _____

Common Preposition/Adjective Combinations:
Angry at, Mad at, Happy with, Pleased with, Scared of, Afraid of

Read the explanation, and study the examples. Complete the exercises that follow.

Explanation 46: Use <u>at</u> with <u>mad</u> and <u>angry</u>, <u>with</u> with <u>happy</u> and <u>pleased</u>, and <u>of</u> with <u>afraid</u> and <u>scared</u>.

| mad <u>at</u> | happy <u>with</u> | afraid <u>of</u> |
| angry <u>at</u> | pleased <u>with</u> | scared <u>of</u> |

Exercise J3

Complete the sentences logically according to Explanation 46.

1. If you talk during the movie, people will get _____ you.

2. I don't believe in ghosts, but I'm _____ them!

3. Harriet's parents were very _____ her when she got straight As in school.

4. Many people are _____ snakes.

5. The new office worker is very efficient, and the boss is quite _____ her.

Putting It Together

Match the words on the left with the words on the right, and write sentences using what you have learned in Explanation 46. Use <u>because</u> and one of the preposition/ adjective combinations from the explanation in each sentence. The first one has been done for you as an example.

☑ 1. Gary's parents   ☐ a. The Jones didn't invite them to their party.

☐ 2. Marsha's mother   ☐ b. She cleaned the whole house.

☐ 3. Most people   ☐ c. They are very poisonous.

☐ 4. The Smiths   ☑ d. He took the car without asking.

1. *Gary's parents are angry at him because he took the car without asking.* _____

2. _____

_____

3. _____

_____

4. _____

_____

Common Preposition/Adjective Combinations: *Get/Be Used to, Get/Be Accustomed to*

Read the explanation, and study the examples. Complete the exercises that follow.

> **Explanation 47:** Use <u>to</u> with <u>get/be used</u> to and <u>get/be accustomed</u> to mean to get or be familiar enough with something that it seems usual or ordinary.
>
> I'll never <u>get used to</u> the hot weather here.
>
> Many students were late because they <u>weren't accustomed to</u> getting up so early.

Exercise J4

Prepositions almost always go before nouns. Write the preposition <u>to</u> in the blank. Then check the correct *-ing* noun (gerund) and write it in the blank.

❐ **working**   ❐ **doing**   ❐ **speaking**   ❐ **eating**   ❐ **listening**

1. Mr. Jones is sleepy because he isn't used _____ the midnight shift at the factory.

2. The cafeteria serves dinner at nine. I'm hungry because I'm not accustomed _____ so late.

3. Maria wrote home to her parents in Mexico that she was finally getting used _____ English every day.

4. When Harold went to college, he had to get used _____ his own laundry.

5. When the rock band began to play, some people left because they weren't accustomed _____ to such loud music.

Putting It Together

Paraphrase (write in different words) the following sentences using what you have learned in Explanation 47.

1. Randy can't finish the enchilada because he has never eaten Mexican food before.

   _____

2. I don't feel comfortable speaking English because I don't do it very often.

   _____

3. We're tired. We almost never work this hard!

   _____

4. Cold weather doesn't bother me because I have lived in the North all my life.

   _____

5. Kate grew up in New York City, so the traffic and noise seem ordinary to her.

   _____

Beyond the Explanations

The meaning of <u>get used to</u> or <u>be used to</u> in Explanation 47 is very different from the meaning of the verb <u>use to</u>. <u>Use to</u> is always used in the simple past tense. It means that something happened regularly in the past but does not happen now.

<u>Be/Get Used to</u> (as in Explanation 47):

> <u>I'm used to</u> eating dinner at 6:00 sharp. (This seems ordinary or normal.)

> Harriet has finally <u>got used to</u> living in the city. (This seems ordinary or normal.)

<u>Use to</u>:

> I <u>used to</u> work in a bank, but I'm retired now. (This happened regularly in the past but does not happen now.)

> When Shirley was a child, she <u>used to</u> eat a lot of candy. (This happened regularly in the past but does not happen now.)

✓ Quick Check 18

Check the sentences in which an action happened regularly in the past but does not happen today.

❏   1.   I <u>got used to</u> spicy food when I lived in Mexico, and I still like it today.

❏   2.   I <u>used to</u> speak French every day when I lived in Quebec.

❏   3.   The Crawleys <u>used to</u> live in Indiana, but they moved to Texas last year.

❏   4.   Mary <u>is used to</u> the thin air in Mile High City.

❏   5.   When I was a child my mother <u>used to</u> tie my shoes for me.

Exercise J5

Check a preposition and a noun. Write them in the blanks to complete the sentences logically. The first one has been done as an example.

☑ **about**   ❏ **to**   ❏ **with**   ❏ **with**   ❏ **on**

❏ **my neighbors**   ☑ **failing**   ❏ **the cold weather**   ❏ **the murder**

❏ **the subject**

1.   Jennifer studies hard, so she never has to worry _____*about failing*_____.

2.   I'm not happy _____ because their dog barks late at night.

3.   Jim likes his new home in Alaska, but he's still not used _____.

4.   My client is innocent. He had nothing to do _____.

5.   Glenn got interested in archaeology, so he bought a book _____.

Exercise J6

Write the letter of the INCORRECT part of the sentence in the blank. Then write that part the way it should be, as shown in the example. Write ø if no preposition is needed.

Incorrect: Should Be:

_____C_____   _____in_____   I read a book <u>on</u> history while I was <u>on</u> vacation <u>at</u> England.
                A   B   C

Incorrect: Should Be:

1. _____ _____ I went <u>to</u> a trip <u>to</u> Europe <u>in</u> 1978.
             A   B   C

2. _____ _____ The cook went <u>out</u> the kitchen <u>for</u> a minute and then came back <u>in</u>.
                 A   B   C

3. _____ _____ <u>Since</u> his graduation <u>from</u> college, John's parents have been very
             A   B

                happy <u>at</u> him.
                   C

4. _____ _____ I wrote a letter <u>to</u> home in which I talked <u>about</u> what I would do
                   A   B

                <u>on</u> spring break.
                C

5. _____ _____ It's dark <u>in</u> this room. Could you turn the lights <u>off</u> <u>for</u> me?
                A   B C

Prepositions in Context

Read the following letter that Ricky Barton wrote to his parents while he was away at school. Answer the questions that follow using the correct prepositions. Write ø if no preposition is needed. Then read the letter again to correct your work.

Ricky Barton's Letter Home (Part 1)

August 27, 2005

Dear Mom and Dad,

In general, school so far is fine, but yesterday one of the professors did something that I didn't agree with. He handed out a piece of paper that looked something like this:

Name _____

Complete the sentences.
(You may use the list below the sentences.)
1. The study of zoos is called _____.
2. If I wanted to study meteors, I would study _____.
3. _____ is the study of dinosaurs.

archaeology
zoology
meteorology

After a few minutes, we handed the papers back in and the professor looked at them. Then he laughed at us. "Well," he said. "John Smith says that the study of zoos is called zoology. Mr. Smith, you are wrong! Zoology is the study of <u>animals</u>. Not zoos. You don't seem to know very much, do you?"

The class got very quiet. Nobody was used to such rude behavior— especially from a professor. The professor didn't notice the reaction, though. He just went on talking.

"Who's Mary Jones?" he asked. "Ah, good afternoon, Miss Jones. Do you really think that meteorologists study meteors? Well, they don't. Meteorologists study the <u>weather</u>. All educated people know that. Meteorology has nothing to do with meteors!"

Mary Jones didn't answer him. She seemed to be angry at him. I thought she might get up and walk out of the classroom.

Finally, I heard my own name. "Ricky Barton, you should know that archaeology has nothing to do with dinosaurs. Archaeologists study the <u>people</u> of the past. Dinosaurs and people did not live together.

> *So why would an archaeologist study dinosaurs? You certainly don't know much about archaeology, do you?"*
>
> *I felt really foolish. The professor had tricked me. I was angry too because I thought it was wrong to teach people by making fun of them. I'm not pleased with that professor at all.*

1. What did the professor do first?

    He handed _____ a paper.

2. Where was the list of subjects?

    The list was _____ the sentences.

3. What did the students do?

    They handed the papers back _____.

4. What did the professor do next?

    He looked _____ the papers and laughed _____ the students.

5. Why did the class get quiet?

    They were not used _____ such rude behavior—especially _____ a professor.

6. Did the professor notice that everyone was quiet?

    Apparently not; he just went _____ talking.

7. Is meteorology about meteors?

    No, it has nothing to do _____ them.

8. How did Mary Jones seem to Ricky?

    She seemed angry _____ the professor, and he thought that she might walk _____ _____ the class.

9. What did the professor say about Ricky?

    He said Ricky didn't know much _____ archaeology.

10. What did Ricky think was wrong?

    Teaching people _____ making fun of them.

11. How does Ricky feel about the professor?

    He's not pleased _____ him ____ all.

Ricky Barton's Letter Home (Part 2)

> On a happier note, our geology class went out of town on a field trip to Red Mountain on Saturday. The whole class went together on a bus, so I was able to take advantage of this and get acquainted with some of the other students. We spent most of our time looking for crystals of augite, a black mineral. (If you're not familiar with augite, don't feel bad. Our textbook has only one paragraph on it!)
>
> We didn't arrive back at the university until 6:00. It was a long, tiring trip, but I know I will look back on it with a lot of pleasure someday.
>
> Well, I'm going to drop this letter into the mailbox and go to bed. I'm looking forward to hearing from you, and I'll see you on semester break.
>
> Love,
>
> Ricky
>
> PS: Thanks for the 20 bucks!

1. What did the geology students do?

    They went _____ _____ town _____ a field trip _____ Red Mountain _____ Saturday.

2. How did they go?

    They went _____ a bus.

3. What was Ricky able to do?

    He was able to take advantage _____ the trip and get acquainted _____ some of the students in his class.

4. What did the students do at Red Mountain?

    Most _____ the time they spent looking _____ crystals _____ augite.

5. Does their text say much about augite?

    No, it has only one paragraph _____ it.

6. When did they get back?

    They didn't arrive back _____ the university _____ 6:00.

7. Someday what will Ricky do?

He'll look back _____ the trip with pleasure.

8. What was the last thing Ricky did after he wrote the letter?

He dropped the letter _____ the mailbox and went _____ bed.

9. How does Ricky close the letter?

He tells his parents that he looks forward _____ hearing from them and that he will see them _____ semester break.

10. Why does he thank them?

He thanks them _____ the $20 that they sent him.

Common Preposition/Adjective Combinations: *Composed of, Made of, Made from*

Read the explanation, and study the examples. Complete the exercises that follow.

Explanation 48: Use <u>made of</u> or <u>composed of</u> to indicate <u>composition</u> and <u>made from</u> to indicate <u>source</u> or <u>physical change</u>.

This fork is <u>made of</u> silver.   (composition)

Aspirin is <u>made from</u> petroleum.   (source or physical change)

Most parts of cars are <u>made of</u> metal.   (composition)

Steel is <u>made from</u> iron ore.   (source or physical change)

Water is <u>composed of</u> hydrogen and oxygen.   (composition)

Exercise J7

Write <u>from</u> in the blank if the noun that follows it is the source. Write <u>of</u> if the noun that follows it is the composition.

1. If you touch your desk, are you touching a tree?

   No, the desk is made _____ wood.

2. If you touch wood, are you touching a tree?

   No, wood is a material made _____ trees.

3. When people eat cheese are they eating milk?

   No, they are eating cheese. Cheese is made _____ milk. It isn't made _____ milk.

4. Why is your ring so valuable?

   It's made _____ gold.

5. What kind of shoes are you wearing?

   Tennis shoes. They're made _____ rubber.

6. What is rubber?

   It's a material made _____ the sap of rubber trees.

7. H_2SO_4 is the formula for sulfuric acid, an acid composed _____ hydrogen, sulfur, and oxygen.

8. Glass is made _____ sand.

Prepositions in Context

Read the story about what happened to the Medford family while they were on a car trip last year. Answer the questions that follow using the correct prepositions. Write ø if no preposition is needed. Then read the story again to correct your work.

The Thunderstorm on the Medfords' Car Trip

Boom! Boom! BOOM! Lightning crashed along the highway and the rain, illuminated by the car's headlights, swept across the road. Michael Medford slowed the car down. "What a thunderstorm!" he remarked. "I don't like lightning; I'm afraid of it. I don't think I'll ever get used to it."

"That lightning was pretty close to us," complained Martha Medford. "I hope it doesn't hit the car."

Don't worry about that, " said Michael. "Our tires are made of rubber so we're safe in the car."

"Uh, you're wrong about that, Dad," came a voice from the back seat. It was the Medfords' son, Randy.

"Wrong about what, son?"

"About rubber tires and lightning," said Randy. "I read a book on lightning. Rubber tires don't protect people from lightning."

"You mean we're not safe in the car?" asked his father.

"We're safe, Dad, but it's because we're surrounded by metal. Rubber tires have nothing to do with it."

Michael Medford was quiet for a moment. Then he said, "I guess that means I was wrong to have gone fishing in that thunderstorm last summer."

"You went fishing in a thunderstorm?" Randy asked.

"Yes, I did," admitted Michael. "I was wearing tennis shoes made of rubber. I thought I was safe."

"Dad, rubber tennis shoes offer no protection at all. Lightning is much too powerful. It has no respect for your tennis shoes!"

"I guess you're right, son," said Michael.

"I told you so," said Martha.

1. From the title, when did the storm happen?

   It happened _____ the Medfords' car trip.

2. Where did the lightning crash?

   _____ the highway

3. Why could the Medfords see the rain?

   It was illuminated _____ the headlights.

4. Does Michael Medford like lightning?

   No, he's afraid _____ it and thinks he will never get used _____ it.

5. What does Martha Medford complain about?

   She complains about the lightning's being _____ _____ them.

6. Why does Michael Medford think they are safe?

   The car's tires are made _____ rubber.

7. What does Randy say?

   He says he read a book _____ lightning and that his father is wrong _____ rubber tires.

8. Does Randy say they are safe?

   Yes, he says they are safe _____ the car, but rubber tires have nothing to do_____ it. They offer no protection _____ all.

9. Why are they safe?

   They are surrounded _____ metal.

10. What does Michael Medford admit?

    He admits that he went fishing in a thunderstorm while he was wearing tennis shoes made _____ rubber.

Putting It Together

Match a word on the left with a word on the right, and write sentences using what you have learned in Explanation 48. The first one has been done as an example.

     ☑   1. chair   ☐ a. glass

     ☐   2. wood   ☐ b. cloth

     ☐   3. shirt   ☐ c. cocoa beans

     ☐   4. windows   ☐ d. trees

     ☐   5. chocolate   ☐ e. wheat

     ☐   6. bread   ☑ f. wood

1. *My chair is made of wood.* _____

2. _____

3. _____

4. _____

5. _____

6. _____

EXPANSION EXERCISES FOR CHAPTER 5

Complete the following assignments to expand on what you have learned in Chapter 5.

1. Write a sentence telling what a movie, book, song, or story is about. Use the verb <u>have to do with</u>.

2. Review Explanations 42 and 44 and the exercises that follow them. Write sentences for each of the multi-word verbs in the explanations.

3. Write three sentences with each of the following: <u>angry at</u>, <u>happy with</u>, <u>afraid of</u>.

4. Write about something you used to do but don't do anymore.

5. Write about something that you got used to (accustomed to, familiar with).

6. Write sentences to tell what things are composed of, made of, or made from.

COMPREHENSIVE TEST 5

Write the correct preposition in the space according to what you have learned. If none is needed, write ø in the space.

1. Henry is mad _____ his brother because he wouldn't help him with his homework.

2. My neighbor is always borrowing things _____ me and never returning them.

3. I'm sorry; Andrew Reardon is not in New York; he left _____ the West Coast.

4. King Tut's mask is made _____ pure gold.

5. There's a traffic light on 1st Street, and 3rd Street is two blocks _____ that.

6. The customer stood _____ the counter and paid for his groceries.

7. Most medicines are made _____ plants.

8. My grandfather can't hear well, so I often have to repeat myself _____ him.

9. Glenn Miller was the leader _____ a popular orchestra.

10. After the operation, the doctors took _____ their rubber gloves.

11. A politician must be very good _____ public speaking.

12. Many people are moving _____ the country and into the cities.

13. Margaret Mead wrote a book _____ her observations in Samoa.

14. _____ the 20th century, the airplane was only a dream.

15. All the students said that they would come, but nobody showed _____.

16. I live on the northwest corner of Main Street and Elm, and you are on the southeast. We live _____ each other.

17. After the baseball game, my muscles hurt. I wasn't used _____ playing so hard!

18. Diane isn't in; she went _____.

19. We loved our trip to the mountains, and we are looking forward _____ going back.

20. The hunter walked toward the deer, and the deer ran _____ him.

21. This tree was planted _____ my great grandmother.

22. Many students come to school _____ bikes.

23. Abraham Lincoln was married _____ Mary Todd Lincoln.

24. The Trentons took more than 1,000 photographs when they were _____ their trip to Africa.

25. What does geography have to do _____ politics? A lot.

26. The President arrived _____ Vancouver on October 12.

27. Our biggest store is located _____ downtown.

28. Ned needs to buy a new ink cartridge _____ his printer.

29. All of the students in this class should study _____ an hour at home every day.

30. When I was a child, I used to be afraid _____ the dark.

ANSWERS TO EXERCISES IN CHAPTER 5

I1: 1. on 2. off 3. off 4. on, off 5. on, off 6. off, on 7. off, on 8. on, off 9. on, off 10. on, on

Quick Check 16: Check sentences 1 and 3. 1. into 2. in 3. into 4. in

I2: 1. into (or in), out 2. into (or in) out 3. out, into (or in) 4. into (or in), out 5. into (or in), out

Quick Check 17: Check sentences 1, 4, and 5. 1. out of 2. out 3. out 4. out of 5. out of

I3: 1. take advantage of 2. get along with 3. look back on 4. look forward to 5. get along 6. look forward to 7. look back on 8. take advantage of

I4: 1. look forward greatly to 2. look back happily on 3. get along wonderfully with

I5: 2. off 3. in 4. into 5. in 6. out 7. of 8. up 9. on 10. on 11. on 12. along 13. to 14. for

I6: 2. on, picnic 3. on, trip 4. on (a) vacation 5. on, break

J1: 2. with mathematics 3. with rocks and minerals 4. with prehistoric people 5. with the crime 6. with your radio

J2: 1. about 2. about 3. about 4. on or about 5. about or on

J3: 1. mad at or angry at 2. afraid of or scared of 3. happy with or pleased with 4. afraid of or scared of 5. happy with or pleased with

J4: 1. to working 2. to eating 3. to speaking 4. to doing 5. to listening

Quick Check 18: Check sentences 2, 3, and 5.

J5: 2. with my neighbors 3. to the cold weather 4. with the murder 5. on the subject

J6: 1. A, on 2. A, out of 3. C, with 4. A, ø 5. B, on

J7: 1. of 2. from 3. from, of 4. of 5. of 6. from 7. of 8. from

CHAPTER 6

Prepositions for Cause and Effect and Opinion

PART K: Explanations 49–54
Prepositions that Join Other Words to Act as Adverbs: *at first*

Read the explanation, and study the examples. Complete the exercises that follow.

Explanation 49: Use <u>at first</u> to show that something begins one way but changes later. <u>At first</u> goes with a clause (a subject and a verb). It is often followed by <u>but</u> or <u>however</u>. These words help to show that something changes or becomes different.

Example 1: <u>At first,</u> I didn't like the food here, <u>but</u> I do now.

Example 2: <u>At first,</u> I didn't like the food here. <u>However,</u> I do now.

Note: Example 2 with <u>However</u> has two sentences, while Example 1 with <u>but</u> has only one sentence.

Exercise K1

Fill in the blanks with <u>at first</u> and <u>but</u> or <u>However</u> according to what you have learned from Explanation 49.

1. _____, I didn't understand modern jazz, _____ I really like it now.

2. _____, I didn't agree with the rules. _____, after Brian Hamilton explained them to me, I changed my mind.

3. _____, Terry Dale didn't want to learn the computer. _____, now she couldn't live without it.

4. _____, I liked reading mystery novels, _____ now I'm tired of them.

Prepositions in Context

Read the story that Jeff Baker wrote about his experiences playing the piano. Answer the questions that follow using the correct prepositions. Write ø if no preposition is needed. Then read the story again to correct your work.

The Life of the Party

Something that seems difficult at first can later become easy. I learned this when my father taught me how to play the piano. He said, "Learn how to play, and you'll always be invited to parties." He was right, of course, but I had a problem. I was very shy, and at first I could not play in front of people at all. I was too scared. Instead of worrying about being left out, I worried about getting *invitations* to parties! Everyone wanted me to come and play, and I was miserable. As the years passed, however, I slowly became accustomed to playing for people at parties, and now I look forward to those invitations. Most Saturday nights, you can find me sitting at the piano in someone's living room thankful for my father's music lessons and wise advice.

1. Do difficult things always stay difficult?

   No, something that seems difficult _____ first can become easy later on.

2. How well did Jeff Baker play for people at first?

   Not very well. In fact, _____ first he couldn't play in front of people _____ all.

3. Was he afraid of not being invited?

   No, he didn't worry _____ being left _____; _____ first, he worried _____ being *invited* to parties!

4. Is Jeff Baker afraid of getting invitations now?

   Not at all. Now, he looks forward _____ getting them because he has become accustomed _____ playing the piano _____ people _____ parties.

5. On Saturdays, where can Jeff Baker often be found?

   _____ the piano _____ someone's living room.

Putting It Together

Complete the sentences according to what you have learned in Explanation 49.

1. At first, _____, but now I am used to it.

2. I am accustomed to _____ now, but at first I _____
   _____.

3. At first, some people _____. However, after
   they get familiar with it, they _____.

Beyond the Explanations

At first and first are different in meaning. As explained in Explanation 49, at first is usually used to describe something that begins a certain way but changes later. First, however, is used to list steps, events, or ideas.

Correct:	1. At first, people thought the world was flat, but later they learned that it was round. (something that began a certain way but changed)
Correct:	2. First, make the coffee. Second, cook the bacon. Last, fry the eggs. (a list of steps)
Correct:	3. The scientist explained his theory to us. First, he told us how he developed the theory. Then he told us how he tested it. (a list of events or ideas)

Note that in #2 and #3 the steps and events are listed, but nothing changes. In #1, people began thinking that something was true but later changed their minds.

Quick Check 19

Check the sentences in which something begins a certain way but *changes*. Write <u>at first</u> in the checked sentences. Then write <u>first</u> in all the other sentences.

☐ 1. _____, Cindy's parents didn't like her new husband, but now they do.

☐ 2. I couldn't understand algebra _____, but now I think it's easy.

☐ 3. Here's how to study. _____, relax. That's really important.

☐ 4. The movie star said, "I have so much to say! _____, I would like to thank my fans."

☐ 5. _____, the baseball team was not very good. However, in a few months they became the best in the country.

☐ 6. Grace has a list of things to do, but she doesn't know which to do _____.

Putting It Together

Write a short paragraph on a separate piece of paper that lists events using the paragraph structure that follows. Of course, you may write more sentences if you wish. You can also change the word *unusual* to the word *normal*.

Yesterday was an unusual day. First, _____ _____. Then _____. Finally, _____.

Common Preposition/Noun Combinations: *Effect on*

Read the explanation, and study the examples. Complete the exercises that follow.

> **Explanation 50:** Use <u>effect on</u> to show how one thing affects another.
>
> The moon has an <u>effect on</u> the ocean's tides.
>
> The <u>effect</u> of pesticides <u>on</u> birds is well known.

Exercise K2

For each sentence, check two of the items below. Write them in the logical blank with the words <u>effect on</u>. The first one has been done as an example.

- ☑ **smoking**
- ☐ **sun**
- ☐ **drug**
- ☐ **mercy**
- ☐ **the cruel king**
- ☐ **your skin**
- ☑ **a person's lungs**
- ☐ **the patient's condition**

1. *Smoking* has a bad *effect on a person's lungs*.

2. The doctors gave a new _____ to the patient, and immediately there was a positive _____.

3. The people's cries for _____ had no _____.

4. You shouldn't stay out in the bright _____ because the _____ _____ could be very bad indeed.

One-Word Prepositions: *up, down*

Read the explanation, and study the examples. Complete the exercises that follow.

Explanation 51: Use <u>up</u> and <u>down</u> to show an increase or a decrease in height, number, or quantity as in the illustration below.

up ↑   down ↓

The spider climbed <u>up</u> and <u>down</u> the wall. (height)

Since last year, the price of oil has steadily gone <u>up</u>. (quantity)

As more policemen are hired, the number of crimes goes <u>down</u>. (number)

Exercise K3

Review Explanations 50 and 51. Write the correct prepositions in the blanks.

1. Does smoking have an effect _____ cancer rates? Yes, as more people smoke, cancer rates go _____.

2. The police chief wanted to know what kind of effect his work had _____ the crime rate. He was happy to learn that the crime rate was _____.

3. What effect does a bad cold have _____ the body? First, the temperature of the body usually goes _____.

4. Jim Yuma took some medicine for his high blood pressure. The effect _____ his condition was excellent. Today his blood pressure is _____.

Putting It Together

Part A

Fill the blanks with <u>on</u>, <u>up</u>, or <u>down</u>.

1. *Question:* What is the effect of altitude _____ air temperature?
   Answer: As altitude increases, the temperature of the air goes _____.

2. *Question:* Does the number of dry days have an effect _____ the possibility of forest fires?
   Answer: Yes, when there have been a lot of dry days, the danger of forest fires goes _____.

3. *Question:* What does depth have to do with water pressure?
   Answer: As depth increases, water pressure goes _____.

4. *Question:* Does the number of absences have an effect _____ a student's grades?
   Answer: Yes, as absences go _____, grades go _____.

Part B

Draw a graph like the one that follows for #2, #3, or #4. Write a title above your graph. Use the word <u>effect</u> and the preposition <u>on</u> in your title.

Example:

The Effect of Altitude on the Temperature of the Air

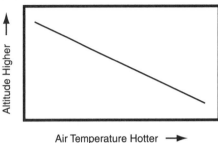

Air Temperature Hotter ➡

Common Preposition/Verb Combinations: *Result in*

Read the explanation, and study the examples. Complete the exercises that follow.

> **Explanation 52:** Use <u>result in</u> to mean <u>cause</u>.
>
> War <u>results in</u> widespread death and destruction.
>
> Smoking <u>results in</u> hundreds of thousands of deaths each year.

Exercise K4

Match the cause on the left with the related effect on the right. The first one has been done as an example.

Matching Exercise

Causes		Effects
1. increasing altitude	*C*	a. a lower crime rate
2. exposure to the sun	____	b. skin cancer
3. good police work	____	c. lower temperatures
4. frequent exercise	____	d. a healthier heart
5. hurricanes	____	e. damage to coastal cities

Now complete these sentences by writing the correct preposition and the correct effect in the blank. The first one has been done as an example.

6. Does increasing altitude have an effect <u>*on*</u> temperature?

   Yes, increasing altitude results <u>*in*</u> <u>*lower temperatures*</u> .

7. Does exposure to the sun have an effect _____ your health?

   Yes, excessive exposure to the sun can result _____ _____ .

8. What can good police work result _____?

   Good police work can result _____ _____ .

9. Can frequent exercise result _____ _____?

   Yes, exercise has many such beneficial effects _____ the body.

10. What effect can hurricanes have _____ cities on the coast?

    Hurricanes can result _____ _____ .

Putting It Together

Write three causes and the three effects that go with them. Then for each cause and effect write a sentence using <u>result in</u>.

_____

_____

_____

Common Preposition/Verb Combinations: *Object to, Insist on*

Read the explanation, and study the examples. Complete the exercises that follow.

> **Explanation 53:** Use <u>object to</u> to mean strongly oppose and <u>insist on</u> to mean demand.
>
> I very much <u>object to</u> your plans to raise my rent.
>
> At the restaurant, John <u>insisted on</u> a better table.

Exercise K5

Review Explanation 53. Fill in the blanks with the correct prepositions.

1. Our company insists _____ the highest quality in everything we produce.

2. I object _____ the senator's comments. I think they are unfair.

3. No one objects _____ your asking a question, but you must raise your hand first.

4. Bob Cratchit, you're late again. I insist _____ punctuality!

Exercise K6

Fill in the blanks with the correct prepositions. Change the verb in parentheses to a noun by adding *-ing*. Write it with the correct possessive adjective (*my, your, his, her, their, our*). The first one has been done as an example.

1. I whispered to Diane in class. The teacher didn't like it. She said, "I strongly object
   to your whispering to each other in class!
   (whisper)

2. Carl Harrison was late to work three days in a row. His boss told him that he insisted
   _____ at work on time.
   (arrive)

3. The Simons' 17-year-old daughter went to a Saturday night dance and, her parents insisted _____ home by 11:00.

           (come)

4. We all lit up cigarettes in the hall after class. One of the other students objected _____, so we had to go outside.

       (smoke)

Putting It Together

Part A

Write a sentence telling whether or not you object to each of the following.

> *You see:*   drinking and driving
>
> *You write:*   <u>Yes, I object to drinking and driving</u>.

1. anyone's talking in a theater

   _____

2. drivers who go too fast

   _____

3. people who smoke at home

   _____

4. helping a friend

   _____

5. having to do homework

   _____

Part B

Read the sentences and put a check by a person's name. Think of what the person might insist on. Finally, write a sentence with <u>insist on</u>. The first one has been done as an example.

☑ William Tate   ❏ a refund of the money she paid

❏ Laura Reed   ❏ an investigation of the death

❏ Larry Johnson   ☑ their leaving on time

❏ Inspector Price   ❏ better attendance from his students

1. William Tate's employees leave work ten minutes early every day.

   I think he might insist on their leaving on time.

2. Laura Reed bought a radio, and the radio doesn't work.

   _____

3. Half of Larry Johnson's students didn't come to class on Friday.

   _____

4. Inspector Price doesn't think that the death was an accident.

   _____

Common Preposition/Noun Combinations:
Objection to, Insistence on

Read the explanation, and study the examples. Complete the exercises that follow.

Explanation 54: The noun forms of the verbs in Explanation 53 use the same prepositions.

> People seldom have any <u>objection to</u> getting a raise in salary.
>
> I don't understand your <u>insistence on</u> a cash payment. Why can't I write a check?

Exercise K7

Fill in the blanks according to what you have learned in Explanation 54.

1. The company president's _____ high salaries for his employees made him very popular.

2. The company president's _____ high salaries for his employees made him very unpopular.

3. Do you have any _____ my leaving a little early today? I have to go to the dentist.

Beyond the Explanations

The verb <u>affect</u> can be used to carry the meaning of the noun <u>effect</u>. No preposition is necessary. Examples:

> The music had no <u>effect on</u> me.
>
> or
>
> The music did not <u>affect</u> me.

Exercise K8

Rewrite these sentences using the verb <u>affect</u>.

1. Pollution has an effect on lakes and rivers.

2. Does TV violence have an effect on viewers?

_____

_____

Beyond the Explanations

<u>Insist that</u> can be used to carry the meaning of <u>insist on</u>. A clause (a subject and a verb) instead of simply a noun follows <u>insist that</u>. Also, the <u>simple</u> form of the verb is almost always used after <u>insist that</u>.

Examples:

>   Mr. Bender <u>insisted on our arriving</u> at work on time.
>
>   or
>
>   Mr. Bender <u>insisted that we arrive</u> at work on time.
>
>
>   Norman's parents <u>insisted on his taking</u> piano lessons.
>
>   or
>
>   Norman's parents <u>insisted that he take</u> piano lessons.

<u>Note</u>: In the last example, the simple from of the verb <u>take</u> is written instead of <u>takes</u>.

Exercise K9

Rewrite these sentences using <u>insist that</u> and the simple form of the verb.

1. The judge insisted on my answering his question.

   _____

2. I really must insist on Mary's doing her own homework.

   _____

3. The superintendent insisted on our not smoking in the hallways.

   _____

Exercise K10

Write the letter of the INCORRECT part of the sentence in the blank. Then write that part the way it should be as shown in the example.

Incorrect: Should Be:

____*C*____   ____*on*____ Looking <u>back on</u> my days <u>in</u> Ohio has a calming effect <u>in</u> me.
                                    A   B   C

Incorrect: Should Be:

1. _____ _____   <u>First</u>, Kate didn't object <u>to</u> Jay's smoking but later she
                              A   B

   insisted <u>on</u> his stopping.
            C

2. _____ _____   I'm not pleased <u>with</u> you. I must object strongly
                                           A

   <u>to you</u> not showing <u>up at</u> work yesterday.
    B   C

3. _____ _____   Are you familiar <u>about</u> a good mechanic who can
                                            A

   repair the damage <u>to</u> my car <u>for</u> me?
                      B   C

4. _____ _____   Going <u>on</u> vacation <u>in</u> October is my key <u>of</u> happiness.
                                 A   B   C

5. _____ _____   The policeman yelled <u>to</u> the people, "Stay <u>in</u> your
                                                A   B

   houses. A tornado is coming <u>away from</u> us!"
                                C

PART L: Explanations 55–61
Two-Word Verbs and Multi-Word Verbs: *Make Up, Come About, Bring About/On, Come Across, Find Out*

Read the explanation, and study the examples. Complete the exercises that follow.

Explanation 55: The following is a list of common two-word verbs and their definitions. The 🔒 symbol means that the two-word verb is non-separable and no object can go between the two words.

Two-Word Verbs	Definitions
make up	invent something in words
come about	happen
bring about/on	cause
come across 🔒 *	find by chance
find out	learn, discover

*Also sometimes: <u>come by</u> and <u>come upon</u>

Exercise L1

Fill in the blanks with the correct two-word verb according to Explanation 55.

1. The discovery of the prehistoric cave paintings in France was not planned. Someone _____ the paintings by chance.

2. Money is missing from the petty cash box, and the boss is trying to _____ who took it.

3. Greg and Jim are very angry at each other. We all want to find out how this unfortunate disagreement _____.

4. War _____ widespread death and destruction.

5. I told my teacher that I was late because I had a flat tire. The story wasn't true; I just _____ it _____.

Putting It Together

Part A

Paraphrase (say or write in different words) each of these sentences using what you have learned from Explanation 55.

1. I don't believe your story is true.

_____

2. By chance I found an interesting book in the library.

_____

3. William broke a window, and he doesn't want his parents to know about it.

_____

4. Please tell me how this happened.

_____

5. The many recent accidents have caused a demand for new laws.

_____

Part B

Answer one or more of these questions orally or in writing.

1. What did you do as a child that you didn't want your parents to find out about?

2. Did you ever make up a story? Tell why you made it up. Tell whether or not people believed it.

3. Have you ever come across something interesting or valuable? Tell what it was.

Prepositions in Context

Read the newspaper article about Johnny McKay's band, and answer the questions that follow using the correct prepositions. Write ø if no preposition is needed. Then read the article again to correct your work.

LITTLETOWN DAILY NEWS
Friday, May 3, 2004

Johnny and the Sun Dogs
by Brian Cooper

Every now and then a reviewer comes across a really different musical act. That's what happened last Saturday night when I walked into Peabody's Teen Club and listened to Johnny and the Sun Dogs.

At first, I thought I would hear the usual group of young rockers, but I was very wrong. What I saw and heard had a tremendous effect on me.

The Sun Dogs are not afraid of combining their rock and roll with 1940s jazz and swing tunes and even old traditional western songs. But the most impressive thing was the effect their music had on the audience.

Of course, I expected their hot rock songs to bring about cheers and applause. And they did. Their original songs, however, brought on a kind of shocked silence. This interested me very much.

After the show, I asked bass player Brent Morgan about the original songs. "Johnny McKay writes the music for them," said Morgan. "Then he makes up the words. I'm just the bass player. If you want to find out more about those songs, you'll have to talk to Johnny."

By that time, however, the 16-year-old band leader had gone.

Well, I *do* want to find out more about those songs, and if you are curious about the band that everyone seems to be talking about, then go the Peabody's Teen Club on Saturday night. That's where I will be, and I'm looking forward to it very much.

1. What happens every now and then?

   Every now and then a reviewer will come _____ a really different musical act.

2. What did Brian Cooper do?

   He walked _____ Peabody's and listened _____ the Sun Dogs.

3. What did he think would happen?

   _____ first, he thought he would hear something ordinary.

4. Was he right?

   No. What he heard had a tremendous effect _____ him.

5. Are the Sun Dogs afraid to experiment?

   No, they aren't. They're not afraid _____ combining rock and roll with other styles of music.

6. What did their hot rock songs do?

   They brought _____ cheers and applause.

7. How about their original songs?

   They brought _____ a kind of shocked silence from the audience.

8. When did Brian Cooper talk to Brent?

   _____ the show.

9. What did Brent say?

   Brent said that Johnny made _____ the words to the songs. He told Brian to talk _____ Johnny if he wanted to find_____ more about the songs.

10. Did Brian Cooper talk to Johnny?

    No. _____ that time, Johnny had left.

11. What are Brian Cooper's plans?

    He's looking forward _____ going to Peabody's _____ Saturday. He plans to find _____ more about the band that everyone is talking _____.

Prepositions in Context

Read the story about what Sally White found in the desert, and answer the questions that follow using the correct preposition. Write ø if no preposition is needed. Then read the story again to correct your work.

Sally White's Treasure in the Desert

Several years ago, I decided to take a walk in the Sonoran Desert. I drove to the desert, got out of my car, and started walking. An hour later, I was going back to my car. Not far from the road, I saw a flat rock. I was a little tired of walking, so I sat on the rock to rest. Suddenly, next to me on the rock, I saw a small pot made of clay. In it were hundreds of beautiful turquoise beads.

At first, I was so surprised that I couldn't move. I just looked and looked at the pot. I had studied a little about the Southwest, and I knew the pot was very old. It was probably made by the Hohokam Indians, who lived in this desert before Columbus came to America.

Seeing the pot there had a tremendous effect on me. I asked myself how long the pot had sat on the rock. Was it hundreds of years? Thousands? Through the centuries, the pot sat as time passed and the sun and the rain fell down on it. And for all those years not one person had seen it until I came across it by chance. I knew I had to find out more about the pot, so I called the Southwest Museum and told them about it.

Since that day, I have never gone back to look for other pots. As I said, I know that I found my treasure only by chance. I have, however, visited the museum where the pot is in a box under glass. There is a sign that tells the story of the pot. There is also a card next to it that reads, "This ancient Hohokam pot and turquoise beads were found by Sally White on July 22, 1997." Seeing my name printed there in the museum makes me feel very proud.

1. Where did Sally White drive?   She drove _____ the desert.

2. What did she do when she arrived in the desert?   She got _____ her car and started walking.

3. Where was the flat rock?   Not _____ the road.

4. What did she do?   She sat _____ the rock.

5. Why?   She was tired _____ walking.

6. What was on the rock?   _____ her she saw a pot made _____ clay.

7. Was the pot empty?   No, there were beads _____ it.

8. What did she do when she saw the pot?   _____, she was so surprised that she couldn't move. She just looked and looked _____ the pot.

9. Was she excited?   Yes, the effect _____ her was tremendous.

10. Who made the pot and when?   It was probably made _____ the Hohokam Indians _____Columbus came to America.

11. How long had the pot been there?   Hundreds—maybe thousands—of years. _____ the centuries the pot sat on the rock as the sun and rain fell _____ on it.

12. Had other people seen it?   No, _____ all those years no one saw it _____ Sally came _____ it _____ chance.

13. Why did she call the museum?   She wanted to find _____ more about the treasure she had found.

14. Has Sally gone back?   No, _____ that day she has never gone back to look _____ other pots.

15. Where is the pot now?   It's in the Southwest Museum _____ a box _____ glass. Next to it is a card that says that the pot and beads were found _____ Sally White _____ July 22, 1997.

One-Word Prepositions: *between, among*

Explanation 56: Use <u>between</u> to describe something's position in relation to two things and <u>among</u> to describe something's position in relation to three or more things.

The two of us have only 50 cents <u>between</u> us.

The three of us have only 50 cents <u>among</u> us.

The four of us have only 50 cents <u>among</u> us.

Exercise L2

Fill in the blanks with <u>between</u> or <u>among</u> according to Explanation 56.

1. _____ the many students who enrolled at State University was Jennifer, the daughter of the President.

2. There are two mountains to the east. _____ them is Chico, Colorado.

3. Volume B is _____ Volumes A and C.

4. Betty dropped her ring, and it was difficult to find it _____ the hundreds of leaves on the ground.

5. How can we find Carl at the concert? It will be almost impossible to locate him _____ the thousands of other people in the crowd.

Putting It Together

1. Draw a picture of something that is between your home and school, your home and work, or your country and where you are living now. Write sentences with <u>between</u> that go with the picture.

2. Draw a picture of something that is among other things. Write a sentence with <u>among</u> that goes with the picture.

Common Preposition/Verb Combinations: *Prefer* X *to* Y, *Choose* X *over* Y

Read the explanation, and study the examples. Complete the exercises that follow.

Explanation 57: Use <u>to</u> with <u>prefer</u>. Use <u>over</u> with <u>choose</u>.

I <u>prefer</u> pop music <u>to</u> jazz. (prefer X to Y)

Gene always <u>chooses</u> coffee <u>over</u> tea. (choose X over Y)

Exercise L3

Fill in the blanks according to Explanation 57.

1. Do you really prefer grapefruit juice _____ orange juice?

2. If you had a choice, would you choose money _____ a long life?

3. Do most people prefer intelligence _____ beauty when choosing a spouse?

4. Cowboy Joe chose country life _____ life in the big city.

Exercise L4

Review Explanations 56 and 57, and write <u>between</u>, <u>among</u>, <u>over</u>, or <u>to</u> in the spaces.

1. I don't like rain or snow, but if I had to make a choice _____ them, I would choose snow _____ rain.

2. _____ all of the animals in the world, dogs and cats are our favorites. We seem to prefer them _____ the rest.

3. _____ Professor Jackson and Professor Newman, I favor Professor Jackson. I prefer her _____ Professor Newman because she presents information so clearly.

Two-Word Prepositions: *because of, due to*

Read the explanation, and study the examples. Complete the exercises that follow.

> **Explanation 58:** Use <u>of</u> with <u>because</u> and <u>to</u> with <u>due</u> to show a reason.
>
> Everyone wants to go to Hawaii <u>because of</u> its wonderful beaches.
>
> The meeting has been called off <u>due to</u> lack of interest.

Exercise L5

Change the underlined clauses to noun phrases using the cues in parentheses and the information in Explanation 58.

You see: Many people prefer small pickup trucks to cars because <u>they cost less</u>. (their low cost)

You write: Many people prefer small pickup trucks to cars because *of their low cost*.

1. The picnic has been called off because <u>the weather is bad</u>.
   (bad weather)
   The picnic has been called off because _____.

2. Randolf had to repeat his grammar class because <u>he didn't attend regularly</u>.
   (poor attendance)
   Randolf had to repeat his grammar class due _____.

3. No campers are permitted in Entwood Forest because <u>the risk of fire is so great</u>.

(the great fire risk)

No campers are permitted in Entwood Forest because _____

_____.

4. We chose Maria for the job because <u>she is so good at math</u>.

(her excellent math skills)

We chose Maria for the job because _____.

Putting It Together

Change the underlined clause to a noun phrase, and rewrite the sentence.

You see: Several people missed work because <u>they were ill</u>.

You write: Several people missed work because <u>of illness</u>.

1. We have to put off the party until next week because <u>there is another party on the same day</u>.

_____

2. Jan will be late for class today because <u>she had a problem with her car</u>.

_____

3. Lawrence is going to Mexico because <u>he is interested in Aztec history</u>.

_____

4. Amy Rogers doesn't want to go to the mountains because <u>she is afraid of heights</u>.

_____

Exercise L6

Review Explanations 56, 57, and 58. Write <u>between</u>, <u>among</u>, <u>over</u>, <u>to</u>, or <u>of</u> in the blanks.

1. I very much like both movies and books, but if I had to make a choice _____ them, I would choose books _____ movies because _____ their low price and portability.

2. _____ the many students who run for class president, only one can be elected. The voters usually prefer an academic _____ an athlete due _____ the fact that so much written work is necessary in the job of president.

3. _____ manned space flight and unmanned space flight, many scientists favor the latter. They prefer it _____ the former because _____ its low cost.

One-Word Prepositions: *for, against*

Read Explanations 59, 60, and 61. Complete the exercises that follow.

> **Explanation 59:** Use <u>for</u> to show a favorable opinion and <u>against</u> to show an unfavorable opinion.
>
> > Some people are <u>for</u> a 12-month school year. They say it will improve students' education.
> >
> > Some people are <u>against</u> a 12-month school year. They believe students need to go on vacation.

Common Preposition/Adjective Combinations: *Opposed to*

> **Explanation 60:** Use <u>opposed to</u> to show an unfavorable opinion.
>
> > Abolitionists were people who did not believe in slavery. They were <u>opposed to</u> the buying and selling of human beings.

Three-Word Prepositions: *in favor of*

Explanation 61: Use <u>in favor of</u> to show a favorable opinion.

I'm <u>in favor of</u> widening the highway. I think it will make it safer.

Exercise L7

Review Explanations 59, 60, and 61. Write the correct preposition in the blank.

1. Bob's boss is _____ giving him a raise. He doesn't think he deserves one.

2. I was elected president of the club. Out of 20 members, 19 voted _____ me.

3. Few people are _____ higher taxes even though they may be necessary.

4. The workers are very much _____ working next Monday. They say it is a traditional holiday.

Exercise L8

Review Explanations 59, 60, and 61, and choose from among the following to complete each sentence.

for   in favor of   against   opposed to   of   to   on

1. I don't plan to vote for Calvin T. Phillips for City Councilman. I'm very much
   _____ him because _____ his association with known criminals.

2. The members of that club don't want a new ski resort on the mountain. They are very
   much _____ it due _____ its detrimental effects _____ the natural
   beauty of the area.

3. Some of the people in my neighborhood want the new airport. They are very much
   _____ it because _____ its beneficial effects _____ the local economy.

4. Some of the people in my neighborhood don't want the new airport. They are very much
   _____ it because _____ the fear that noise will have a bad effect _____
   the whole area.

Putting It Together

Answer these questions orally or in writing.

1. Make a list of school rules from a school you have attended. Which are you for and which
   are you against? Why?

2. Is there a law that you disagree with? Why are you opposed to the law?

3. Who did you, your parents, or your friends vote for, and why? Who were you (or they)
   against? Why?

Exercise L9

Shelly Martin's composition teacher handed out the following in-class exercise. The students had ten minutes to write a very informal opinion. Check the prepositions as you fill in the blanks in Shelly's composition.

❐ about ❐ against ❐ among ❐ at ❐ between

❐ in ❐ of ❐ of ❐ on ❐ over

Assignment: Imagine this: You are going to establish a colony on another planet, and you have to choose one *grain* to take with you. This is the only grain that the colonists will have to grow on the new planet. Which will it be? Oats, wheat, rice, barley, or corn? Choose only one; there is only room on the spaceship for *one* bag of seeds. Which would you choose? Tell why.

Shelly Martin

Composition Class

Fifth Hour

April 22, 2000

My Choice Is Corn

Most _____ the people I know would probably choose wheat or rice. Indeed, _____ first
   1   2

I was trying to decide _____ those two myself. However, after I thought _____ it, I decided
                          3   4

to choose corn. If you read the label on any food product, you'll find that corn is an ingredient in

almost everything. I'll bet that 90 percent of the packaged food products _____ stores contain
                                                                              5

some form of corn: corn starch, corn syrup, and corn oil. The list goes _____. Corn, wheat,
                                                                            6

and rice are certainly the kings of staple grains, but _____ them only corn is used in so many
                                                          7

products. I have nothing _____ wheat or rice, but I would choose corn _____ them because
                            8   9

_____ its many uses.
   10

EXPANSION EXERCISES FOR CHAPTER 6

Complete the following assignments to expand on what you have learned in Chapter 6.

1. Write a paragraph about something that began one way but changed later. Use <u>at first</u> in your paragraph.

2. Review Quick Check 19 on page 166 and the Beyond the Explanations section on page 165. Write a short paragraph that contains a list of steps for doing something. If you wish, you may use the form that follows.

   It's easy to _____. First, _____
   _____. Second,
   _____
   _____. Finally, _____
   _____.

3. Write about something that had a positive (or negative) effect on your life.

4. Tell why you prefer one thing to another (or why you would choose one thing over another).

5. Write three sentences with <u>because</u> + subject + verb. Rewrite each sentence using <u>because of</u> + noun.

   Examples:

   The movie *Gone with the Wind* made a lot of money because it was popular.

   The movie *Gone with the Wind* made a lot of money because of its popularity.

6. Write a sentence for each of the two-word verbs in Explanation 55.

7. Think of something that you are for or against (in favor of or opposed to). Then write about why you are for or against it.

COMPREHENSIVE TEST 6

Write the correct word in each space provided according to what you have learned. If none is needed, write ø in the space.

1. _____ first Benny couldn't speak Spanish, but now he's very good at it.

2. Alex and Brad couldn't buy the car. They had only $50 _____ them.

3. We don't know who took the money, but we're going to find _____!

4. _____ the 12 people were three teachers and nine students.

5. Acid rain has a bad effect _____ lakes and streams: it kills the fish.

6. I prefer geology _____ sociology.

7. If you have fewer police officers on duty, crime will often go _____.

8. Heavy rains brought _____ widespread flooding.

9. The voters chose Winston Noble _____ Harry Fox just because of his name.

10. The policeman yelled, "Put the gun _____!"

11. By chance I came _____ an old book in the library about my hometown.

12. Two students failed the class due _____ excessive absences.

13. My boss doesn't like my work. He objects _____ everything I do.

14. Our product is selling well because _____ its low price.

15. The trees on Elm Street are beautiful. No one is _____ cutting them down.

16. When Ann got on the plane, she insisted _____ a window seat.

17. Well, hi, Pauline! I haven't seen you _____ last year.

18. No one likes the plan. Everyone is _____ it.

19. Do you have any objection _____ my bringing a friend to class?

20. Not changing the oil in your car can result _____ damage to the engine.

21. Our insistence _____ high quality has made our products very popular.

22. Kelly Griffen wrote a book _____ the fishes of desert lakes.

23. Fictional characters are not real; authors just make them _____.

24. At the end of the race, the crowd shouted, "Go ____! Don't stop now!"

25. "Don't worry _____ me," said the Sheriff. "I'll be all right."

26. I bought two hot dogs _____ the baseball game last Saturday.

27. By studying history we may be able to understand why war comes _____.

28. I often think _____ the summers I spent in Minnesota.

29. Yes, that's a good idea. I'm _____ it!

30. _____ first, my job seemed hard, but I got used to it.

ANSWERS TO EXERCISES IN CHAPTER 6

K1	1. At first, but 2. At first, However 3. At first, However 4. At first, but
Quick Check 19	Check sentences 1, 2, and 5. 1. At first 2. at first 3. First 4. First 5. At first 6. first
K2	2. drug, effect on the patient's condition. 3. mercy, effect on the cruel king. 4. sun, effect on your skin
K3	1. on, up 2. on, down 3. on, up 4. on, down
K4	2. b 3. a 4. d 5. e 7. on, in, skin cancer 8. in, in, a lower crime rate 9. in, a healthier heart, on 10. on, in damage to coastal cities
K5	1. on 2. to 3. to 4. on
K6	2. on his arriving 3. on her coming 4. to our smoking
K7	1. insistence on 2. objection to 3. objection to
K8	1. Pollution affects lakes and rivers. 2. Does TV violence affect viewers?
K9	1. The judge insisted that I answer his question. 2. I really must insist that Mary do her own homework. 3. The superintendent insisted that we not smoke in the hallways.
K10	1. A, At first 2. B, to your 3. A, with 4. C, to 5. C, toward(s) or at
L1	1. came across/by/upon 2. find out 3. came about 4. brings about/on 5. made, up
L2	1. Among 2. Between 3. between 4. among 5. among
L3	1. to 2. over 3. to 4. over
L4	1. between, over 2. Among, to 3. Between, to
L5	1. of bad weather 2. to poor attendance 3. of the great fire risk 4. of her excellent math skills
L6	1. between, over, of 2. Among or Of, to, to 3. Between, to, of
L7	1. against or opposed to 2. for or in favor of 3. for or in favor of 4. against or opposed to
L8	1. against or opposed to, of 2. against or opposed to, to, on 3. for or in favor of, of, on 4. against or opposed to, of, on
L9	1. of 2. at 3. between 4. about 5. in 6. on 7. among 8. against 9. over 10. of

CHAPTER 7

Prepositions for Exemplifying and Comparing/Contrasting

PART M: Explanations 62–67
Prepositions that Join Other Words to Act as Adverbs: *for example, for instance, to begin with, for one thing*

Read the explanation, and study the examples. Complete the exercises that follow.

Explanation 62: Use <u>for example</u>, <u>for instance</u>, <u>to begin with</u>, and <u>for one thing</u> to give examples. They are very similar in meaning.

I try to do a good deed every day. <u>For instance,</u> I often help older people across the street.

Many animals use poison to protect themselves from predators. <u>For example,</u> the toad has poisonous skin.

There are some simple ways to improve the appearance of your house and property. <u>To begin with,</u> you could mow the lawn more often.

I have some good reasons for not being pleased with Mr. Hardy. <u>For one thing,</u> he borrowed $50 from me and never paid it back.

Exercise M1

Check an item in each column and fill in the blanks logically. The first one has been done as an example.

    ☑ **For one**   ☐ **smokes heavily and never exercises**

    ☐ **instance**   ☐ **could start showing up for class regularly**

    ☐ **To begin**   ☑ **have to pack the car**

    ☐ **example**   ☐ **got straight As in all of his classes**

1. There is a lot of preparation to do before a trip. _____*For one*_____ thing, you *have to pack the car.*

2. Jimmy has done some good work at school this year. For _____, he _____.

3. There are several things you could do to improve your grades. _____ _____ with, you _____.

4. Sharon Henderson doesn't have a very healthful lifestyle. For _____, she _____.

Beyond the Explanations

<u>To begin with</u> and <u>For one thing</u> strongly suggest that at least one additional example will soon follow. The word <u>also</u> is often used with the additional example. Additional examples can also follow <u>For instance</u> and <u>For example</u>.

1. This has been a bad week for Margaret. <u>To begin with</u>, she broke her arm. She <u>also</u> <u>caught a bad cold</u>.

2. There are many reasons why Bob is unhappy. <u>For one thing</u>, he has just lost his job. He is <u>also</u> in debt.

3. I travel more than most people. <u>For example</u>, I visited six different countries last year. I <u>also</u> went on several trips to interesting places in my own country.

4. Petroleum has many uses that have nothing to do with cars and transportation. <u>For instance</u>, it is used to make aspirin. It is <u>also</u> a source of chemicals used in soap, plastic, and many other products.

Exercise M2

Write <u>For example</u> or <u>For instance</u> in the first blank. Check an item and fill the next blank logically using the word <u>also</u>. The first one has been done as an example.

☑ taught violin to President Roosevelt

❏ am the captain of my company's soccer team

❏ can learn more about our own planet

❏ put a half gallon of ice cream in the microwave

1. Henry Randleman had a very interesting career as a music teacher. _____*For example*_____, he gave piano lessons to the Queen of England. He *also taught violin to President Roosevelt*.

2. There are some good reasons for exploring space. _____, by doing so, we can begin to understand more about the universe around us. We _____ _____.

3. Sports are an important part of my life. _____, I attend 20 baseball games a year. I _____ _____.

4. My brother has been acting a little strange lately. _____, yesterday he put his school books in the refrigerator. He _____ _____.

Putting It Together

Complete the following logically. In each, use <u>For example</u> or <u>For instance</u> in the second sentence. Use <u>also</u> in the third sentence.

1. Mrs. William's daughter was very helpful last week. For _____, she did the dishes every evening. She _____.

2. My friend Charlie is an excellent worker. For _____, he always arrives at work on time. He _____.

3. I try to live a healthy life. For _____, I _____. I _____.

Beyond the Explanations

For another thing may be written after For one thing to give an additional example as shown below.

1. Why is the teacher displeased with that student? For one thing, he comes to class late every day. For another thing, he never does his homework or pays attention to the lectures.

2. Why did I buy that car? Well, for one thing, it was inexpensive. For another thing, it gets 40 miles per gallon of gasoline.

Exercise M3

Fill the blanks below with <u>For one thing</u> and <u>For another thing</u>.

1. Mrs. Tate is very qualified for the job. _____, she is an excellent writer. _____, she types 100 words a minute on the computer.

2. There are some good reasons that I prefer reading books to going to the theater. _____, you can read a book again and again any time you want. _____, books are often less expensive than theater tickets.

3. I don't want to buy that house. _____, it's too far from the place I work. _____, it's much too big for me.

4. I like this magazine very much. _____, all of the articles are fascinating and well written. _____, it is filled with excellent illustrations.

Prepositions in Context

Read the story, and answer the questions that follow using the correct prepositions. Write ø if no preposition is needed. Then read the story again to correct your work.

Living in Littletown

There are some good reasons why I like living in Littletown. For one thing, it never gets too hot or too cold. That's important to me. For another thing, there is quite a lot to do in the town. Littletown is filled with wonderful shops, art galleries, and museums. You can spend hours just window shopping in Littletown. There are also some very nice natural areas close to town or even in the town itself. For example, the famous Red Pine Forest is just to the north of Littletown, and in the western part of the town there is a beautiful lake where people go swimming, boating, and fishing every day of the year. The night life in Littletown is also quite good. For instance, most evenings there are outdoor concerts where talented musicians play music and people gather to listen or dance. Littletown is not a big city, so at first some people think that it could be boring. However, because of all of the above, they soon find out that this small town is one of the nicest in the country.

1. Why does the writer like Littletown?

    _____ _____ thing, the weather is good. _____ _____ thing, there is a lot to do _____ the town.

2. Are there any natural areas near Littletown?

    Yes. _____ example, the Red Pine Forest is _____ the north of Littletown, and _____ the western part of the town is a beautiful lake.

3. Is the night life good?

    Yes. _____ instance, there are concerts at night.

4. What do some people think of the town?

    _____ first, they think the town might be boring, but because _____ the things the writer talks about, they soon find _____ that Littletown is one _____ the nicest towns _____ the country.

Beyond the Explanations

Two common alternatives to using <u>For example</u> are <u>An example</u> and <u>Some examples</u>. Either can be the subject of a sentence.

1. There are many good singers from England. <u>An example</u> is Sting, who also composes and plays the bass.

2. There are many good singers from England. <u>Some examples</u> are Sting and Paul McCartney, who also compose and play the bass.

Exercise M4

Rewrite the underlined sentences using <u>An example is</u> or <u>Some examples are</u>.

> *You see:*   There are some great places to go in or near Littletown. <u>For example, you can visit the Red Pine Forest</u>.
>
> *You write:*   There are some great places to go in or near Littletown. <u>An example is</u> the Red Pine Forest.

1. There are some great places to go in or near Littletown. <u>For example, you can visit the Red Pine Forest or Lake Gorgeous</u>.

   There are some great places to go in or near Littletown. _____
   _____ the Red Pine Forest and Lake Gorgeous.

2. You can choose from a variety of majors in the university. <u>For example, you can major in engineering</u>.

   You can choose from a variety of majors in the university. _____ engineering.

3. You can choose from a variety of majors in the university. <u>For example, you can major in engineering, biology, or literature</u>.

   You can choose from a variety of majors in the university. _____
   engineering, biology, and literature.

Writing an adjective clause after the noun following <u>An example</u> or <u>Some examples</u> is a common technique for adding information to the sentence.

> There are several stones that are more valuable than diamond. An example is ruby, <u>which is a very hard, red gem</u>.
>
> (adjective clause)

Write <u>An example is</u> or <u>Some examples are</u> in the blank. Then write an adjective clause for the words in parentheses. Write <u>who</u> for people and <u>which</u> for things. The first one has been done as an example.

4. Some great airplanes were produced during World War II. _Some examples are_ the Spitfire, the P-38, and the Mustang, _which are still seen in air shows today._

   (are still seen in air shows today)

5. There are many hobbies that are getting more and more popular.
   _____ bird watching, _____.

   (once was relatively uncommon)

6. Many people have constructed pyramids. _____ the Egyptians and the Aztecs, _____.

   (built hundreds of them)

7. Many drugs are legal in the U.S. _____ alcohol, tobacco, and caffeine, _____.

   (are sold almost everywhere)

8. There have been some wonderful Spanish writers. _____ Cervantes,
   _____.

   (was perhaps the best of all)

Putting It Together

Complete the sentences.

1. I've met some interesting people this year. An example is _____, who
   _____.

2. There are some interesting people in my class. For example, I've just met
   _____, who _____.

3. There are some wonderful places to visit in my country. An example
   _____, which _____.

4. I did some interesting things today. For instance, I _____.
   I also _____.

5. That criminal committed some serious crimes. For example, he
   _____. He also _____.

Exercise M5

In Explanation 19 in Chapter 3, you learned that <u>of</u> can be used to show that one noun (or pronoun) is part of another. Write <u>of</u> in each of the blanks.

1. I have two brothers. One _____ them is married.

2. We have two cars. Both _____ them are small.

3. I read three books. Two _____ them were very good.

4. Mack visited four people. All _____ them gave him a gift.

5. I have met a lot of teachers. Most _____ them were very nice.

6. The Bradys took 100 pictures. Many _____ them were just beautiful.

7. The U.S. imports a lot of oil. Much _____ it comes from Saudi Arabia.

Now combine each of the sentence pairs by changing the pronoun (*them* or *it*) to <u>which</u> or <u>whom</u>. Write <u>which</u> for things and <u>whom</u> for people. Be sure to write only one sentence for each pair. The first two have been done as examples.

8. I have two brothers. One of them is married.

    I have two brothers, one of whom is married .

9. We have two cars. Both of them are small.

    We have two cars, both of which are small .

10. I read three books. Two of them were very good.

    _____

11. Mack visited four people. All of them gave him a gift.

    _____

12. I have met a lot of teachers. Most of them were very nice.

    _____

13. The Bradys took 100 pictures. Many of them were just beautiful.

    _____

14. The U.S. imports a lot of oil. Much of it comes from Saudi Arabia.

    _____

Prepositions that Join Other Words to Act as Adverbs: *in fact*

Read the explanation, and study the examples. Complete the exercises that follow.

Explanation 63: Use <u>in fact</u> to mean <u>indeed</u>.

<u>In fact</u> intensifies or adds emphasis to the sentence before it. The superlative degree (the most, the best, etc.) or a strong example follows <u>in fact</u>.

Dr. Phillips is good at math. <u>In fact</u>, she's <u>the best</u> mathematician in the country.
superlative degree

Hank is familiar with that book. <u>In fact</u>, <u>he wrote it himself</u>.
strong example

Exercise M6

Write <u>In fact</u> in the blank. Then check an item and write it in the logical blank. The first one has been done as an example.

       ❒ no one can read anything he writes

       ❒ it can grow to more than 50 pounds in weight

       ☑ he is one of the most famous in the country

       ❒ they are the largest animals that ever lived

       ❒ she loves it

1. Ray Bradbury is a well-known author. *In fact, he is one of the most famous in the country.*

2. Sharon likes country music. _____, _____

    _____.

3. That doctor has bad handwriting. _____, _____

    _____.

4. The carp is a big fish. _____, _____

    _____.

5. Blue whales are big. _____, _____

    _____.

Putting It Together

Complete the first sentence. Intensify (add emphasis) to the first sentence by writing In fact with the superlative degree or a strong example.

1. My hometown is really _____. In fact, _____.

2. I like _____ very much. In fact, _____.

3. _____ is a very good _____. In fact, _____.

4. _____ is a bad _____. In fact, _____.

5. I'm really interested in _____. In fact, _____.

Common Preposition/Adjective Combinations: *Different from, Similar to*

Read Explanations 64 and 65, and study the examples. Complete the exercises that follow.

Explanation 64: Use <u>different from</u> to show differences and <u>similar to</u> to show similarities.

　　　Poetry is <u>different from</u> music.

　　　Poetry is <u>similar to</u> music.

　　　Dogs are <u>different from</u> cats in many ways.

　　　Dogs are <u>similar to</u> cats in many ways.

Common Preposition/Verb Combinations: *Differ from*

> **Explanation 65:** Use <u>differ from</u> to show differences.
>
> Poetry <u>differs from</u> music.
>
> Dogs <u>differ from</u> cats in many ways.

Exercise M7

Review Explanations 64 and 65, and choose from the words below to complete the sentences. Do not write <u>is</u> or <u>are</u> in the spaces.

different from   similar to   differ(s) from

1. The desert of northern Africa is very _____ the mountains of Switzerland.

2. The temperature at the North Pole is _____ the temperature at the South Pole. Both places are very cold.

3. The color of the sky _____ the color of grass.

4. Angry people _____ happy people in personality.

5. Glenn's accent is _____ Mary's accent because they come from the same part of the country.

Beyond the Explanations

With <u>different</u>, <u>differ</u>, and <u>similar</u>, a preposition is not needed if the two items being compared are written as one subject with <u>and</u>.

A dog is similar <u>to</u> a wolf.	(The preposition <u>to</u> is needed.)
<u>A dog and a wolf</u> are similar.	(Both of the items being compared are written as one subject with <u>and</u>, so no preposition is needed.)
Italian differs <u>from</u> Spanish.	(The preposition <u>from</u> is needed.)
<u>Italian and Spanish</u> differ.	(Both of the items being compared are written as one subject with <u>and</u>, so no preposition is needed.)

Exercise M8

Use <u>and</u> to write the two items being compared as one subject. Rewrite the sentence without the prepositions <u>to</u> or <u>from</u>. The first one has been done as an example.

1. Ice is similar to glass in appearance.

   Ice and glass are similar in appearance.

2. The planet Jupiter is different from the planet Mars.

   _____.

3. This city differs from my hometown.

   _____.

4. Coca-Cola® is similar to Pepsi-Cola®.

   _____.

One-Word Prepositions: *in* to Connect a Quality or Quantity to a Related Noun

Read the explanation, and study the examples. Complete the exercises that follow.

> **Explanation 66:** Use <u>in</u> to connect a quality or quantity to a related noun as illustrated below.
>
> Lake Mono is <u>rather round</u> in <u>shape</u>.
> (quality) (related noun)
>
> Mt. Everest and Death Valley are very <u>different</u> in <u>altitude</u>.
> (quality) (related noun)
>
> That airplane is <u>1,600 pounds</u> in <u>weight</u>.
> (quantity) (related noun)
>
> An apple is red <u>in</u> color.
>
> Tangerines and oranges are similar <u>in</u> taste.
>
> My country is only 300 square miles <u>in</u> area.

Exercise M9

Choose from the following nouns to complete the sentences as in the example.

height   weight   length   width   depth

You see: He is six feet <u>tall</u>.

You write: He is six feet <u>in height</u>.

1. Red Mountain is one mile <u>high</u>.

   Red Mountain is one mile _____.

2. This sheet of paper is eight inches <u>wide</u>.

   This sheet of paper is eight inches _____.

3. Mormon Lake is only one yard <u>deep</u>.

   Mormon Lake is only one yard _____.

4. The Mississippi River is 2,350 miles <u>long</u>.

   The Mississippi River is 2,350 miles _____.

5. How much does that computer <u>weigh</u>?

   This computer is 21 pounds _____.

Exercise M10

Match the words on the left with the most logically related words on the right by writing LETTERS in the spaces. The first one has been done as an example.

1. a circle/a square   _*d*_   a. flavor

2. elephants/ants   _____   b. climate

3. psychology/mineralogy   _____   c. subject

4. spaghetti/sushi   _____   d. shape

5. American deserts/African deserts   _____   e. size

6. snow/cotton   _____   f. color

Review Explanations 64, 65, and 66. Complete the following using the cues in parentheses and the words from the matching exercise above. The first one has been done as an example. <u>Note</u>: Some of the sentences need the prepositions <u>from</u> or <u>to</u> and others don't.

7. Elephants __*are different from*__ ants _____*in size.*_____
               (be different)

8. Elephants and ants _____.
                                 (differ)

9. A circle _____ a square _____.
                 (be different)

10. Psychology and mineralogy _____.
                                   (be different)

11. Spaghetti _____ sushi _____.
                 (differ)

12. American deserts _____ African deserts _____.
                       (be similar)

13. Snow and cotton _____.
                                (be similar)

Prepositions in Context

Read this story, and answer the questions that follow using the correct prepositions. Write ø if no preposition is needed. Then read the story again to check your work.

The Rock from Mars

Part 1

Sixteen million years ago, a huge asteroid or comet struck Mars. The force of the impact was so powerful that rocks from Mars were blasted into space. One of these rocks traveled around the sun for millions of years until it struck the earth about 13,000 years ago. The rock lay in the Antarctic ice until 1984, when it was found by scientists. At that time, no one knew the tremendous effect this discovery would have on the scientific community and the world.

1. How powerful was the impact of the asteroid or comet?

   It was powerful enough to blast rocks _____ Mars _____ space.

2. What did one of these rocks do?

   It traveled _____ the sun _____ millions of years _____ it struck the earth.

3. How long did the rock lie in the ice?

   _____ 1984 when it was found _____ scientists.

4. At that time, did anyone think that the rock might affect the scientific world strongly?

   No. Nobody knew that the rock would have such an effect _____ the scientific world.

Part 2

If one looks at the rock, it does not seem at all impressive at first. It is potato-like in shape, five or six inches in length, and 4.2 pounds in weight. However, scientists know that this rock is very different from most other rocks from space. They know this because of the material it is made of. Gasses in the rock are exactly the same as the gasses in the atmosphere of Mars. (These gasses were measured by the Viking spacecraft in 1976.) Because of this, the scientists know that the rock is from Mars. This means that the rock is very special indeed. In fact, rocks from Mars are some of the rarest objects in the world.

5. Does the rock look special?   No, it doesn't look _____ all impressive ____ first.

6. What does it look like?   It's like a potato ____ shape, and it is about six inches _____ length.

7. How much does it weigh?   It is only about 4.2 pounds _____ weight.

8. Is the rock like other rocks from space?   No, it isn't. It's different _____ them because _____ the material it is made _____.

9. When was the Martian atmosphere measured?   _____ 1976 _____ the Viking spacecraft.

10. Are rocks from Mars rare?   Yes. _____ fact, they are some of the rarest objects in the world.

Part 3

Recently, scientists looked more closely at the rock. What they saw astounded them.
Scientists now have several reasons to believe that the rock contains evidence of life on Mars. For
one thing, there are unusual structures in the rock. These structures are very similar to bacteria
in shape. For another thing, parts of the rock close to the structures are composed of unusual
chemicals, some of which may indicate biological activity. One example is "polycyclic aromatic
hydrocarbons," which often form after organisms die.

11. What happened recently?   Scientists looked _____ the rock again.

12. What evidence for life is there?   _____ _____ thing, there are structures _____ the
                                         rock that are similar _____ shape _____ bacteria.
                                         _____ _____ thing, parts of the rock are
                                         composed _____ unusual chemicals, some _____
                                         which are often produced by biological organisms.

Part 4

Have scientists proved that ancient life existed on Mars? The answer to that question is now
"no." However, the evidence in the rock is strong enough to have brought about a tremendous
amount of interest. In fact, the President of the United States himself announced the news about
the rock on national television in August of 1996. This interest will surely continue, and people
will go on talking about the rock from Mars as scientists try to find out more about it. If the
evidence is verified, it will have a profound effect on the way people look at the world and
themselves.

13. Are we sure about life on Mars?   Right now, the answer _____ that is "no."

14. Are people interested?   Very much so. The rock has brought _____ a great
                                        deal of interest. _____ fact, the President announced
                                        the news _____ the rock himself.

15. What will happen in the future?   People will go _____ talking _____ the rock, and
                                        scientists will try to find ____ more about it.

16. What if the story about life   It will have a profound effect _____ all of us.
     on Mars is true?

Three-Word Prepositions: *with respect to, with/in regard to* to Connect a Quality to a Related Noun or to Mean *about* or *Having to Do with*

Read the explanation, and study the examples. Complete the exercises that follow.

Explanation 67: Use <u>with respect to</u>, <u>with regard to</u>, or <u>in regard to</u> to connect a quality to a related noun or to mean <u>about</u> or <u>having to do with</u>.

My two brothers are very <u>different</u> with respect to <u>personality</u>.
                         quality   related noun

I have some comments <u>with regard to</u> your letter of October 5.
                                 about
                       having to do with

I have some comments <u>in regard to</u> your letter of October 5.
                              about
                     having to do with

Exercise M11

Write <u>with respect to</u> or <u>with/in regard to</u> and the most logical of the following phrases to complete each sentence.

> **his duties as assistant to the superintendent**
>
> **making money**
>
> **your application for the job of office manager**

1. I am writing _____. While you have many excellent qualifications for the job, we have filled the position with another applicant. Best of luck elsewhere!

2. I have nothing but good things to say about this employee. He has always been very professional and diligent _____.

3. This book is entitled *How to Make a Million Dollars,* but there are very few suggestions in it _____.

Exercise M12

Match the words on the left with the most logically related words on the right by writing LETTERS in the spaces. The first one has been done as an example.

1. basketball players/most people   _a_   a. height

2. democrats/Republicans   ____   b. smell

3. roses/onions   ____   c. facial features

4. identical twins   ____   d. use

5. pens/typewriters   ____   e. political viewpoint

Complete the following sentences using the cues in parentheses and the words from the matching exercise. Use <u>with respect to</u> or <u>with/in regard to</u> in each sentence. The first one has been done as an example.

6. Basketball players __*are different from*__ most people ____*with respect to height.*____
   (be different)

7. Basketball players _____ most people _____
   (differ)

   _____.

8. Democrats and Republicans _____
   (be different)

   _____.

9. Roses and onions _____
   (be different)

   _____.

10. Identical twins _____
    (be almost exactly the same)

    _____.

11. Pens _____ typewriters _____
    (be similar)

    _____.

PART N: Explanations 68–74
Prepositions that Join Other Words to Act as Adverbs: *in contrast*

Read Explanations 68 and 69, and study the examples. Complete the exercises that follow.

Explanation 68: Use <u>in contrast</u> to show differences.

> The past tense in English is fairly simple. <u>In contrast</u>, English prepositions can be confusing.
>
> I'm pretty good at most sports. <u>In contrast</u>, I'm very bad at games like chess.

Three-Word Prepositions: *in Contrast to, as Opposed to*

Explanation 69: Use <u>in contrast to</u> and <u>as opposed to</u> to show differences.

> <u>In contrast to</u> lions, lambs are very gentle.
>
> <u>As opposed to</u> small towns, big cities offer the choice of hundreds of restaurants.

Exercise N1

Fill in the blanks in accordance with Explanations 68 and 69.

1. My brother is a world traveler. _____, I'm a homebody who seldom leaves the house.

2. _____ ducks, ostriches cannot fly.

3. _____ typewriters, computers can store written data.

4. E-mail is transmitted electronically. _____, regular mail must be transported physically.

5. _____ ice, which is a solid, water is a liquid.

Beyond the Explanations

Writing an adjective clause after the noun following <u>in contrast to</u> or <u>as opposed to</u> is a common technique for adding information to the sentence.

In contrast to Eric Frank Russell, <u>who wrote science fiction,</u>
adjective clause

Jack London wrote many tales of adventure set in the far
North or in the South Seas.

Exercise N2

Write <u>in contrast to</u> or <u>as opposed to</u> in the blank. Then write an adjective clause for the words in parentheses. Write <u>who</u> for people and <u>which</u> for things. The first one has been done as an example.

1. _____*In contrast to*_____ the Great Basin Desert, *which is sparsely populated* ,
(is sparsely populated)

   some East Coast cities of the U.S. are crowded with people.

2. _____ Al, _____, Eddie is thoughtful.
(is unkind)

3. _____ English spelling, _____,
(can be difficult)

   Spanish spelling is really quite simple.

4. _____ the sailfish, _____,
(grows very large)

the sardine is tiny.

Putting It Together

Use what you have learned in Explanations 68 and 69 to create original sentences.

1. _____. In contrast, _____
   _____.

2. As opposed to _____, who _____,
   _____.

3. In contrast to _____, which _____,
   _____.

4. _____ is very _____ as opposed to_____,
   who _____.

One-Word Prepositions: *like, unlike*

Read the explanation, and study the examples. Complete the exercises that follow.

> **Explanation 70:** Use <u>like</u> to show similarities and <u>unlike</u> to show differences.
>
> > <u>Like</u> the dog, the cat is a popular pet.
> >
> > <u>Unlike</u> the guitar, the violin has only four strings, not six.

Exercise N3

Decide whether <u>like</u> or <u>unlike</u> is needed in the sentence. Then write it with <u>any</u> of the three prepositions shown. The first one has been done as an example.

> **in   with respect to   with/in regard to**

1. England is _*like*_ Australia _*with respect to*_ the language the people speak.

2. Brazil is _____ tiny Luxembourg _____ size.

3. _____ price, a Cadillac is _____ a Ford Escort.

4. _____ general theme, the movie *Rocky* is _____ *Rocky II*. They are very similar.

Beyond the Explanations

Writing an adjective clause after the noun following <u>like</u> or <u>unlike</u> is a common technique for adding information to the sentence.

> Unlike apple juice, <u>which is very sweet</u>, grapefruit juice is rather bitter.
> ⏜
> adjective clause

Exercise N4

Write <u>like</u> or <u>unlike</u> in the sentence. Then write an adjective clause for the words in parentheses. Write <u>who</u> for people and <u>which</u> for things. The first one has been done as an example.

1. __*Unlike*__ cattle, *which eat grass,* wolves are meat eaters.
   (eat grass)

2. _____ the prairie falcon, _____, a chicken can fly only a short distance.
   (is a strong flyer)

3. _____ Alaska, _____, Florida is warm.
   (is cold)

4. _____ my brother, _____, my sister also reads
   (loves literature)

   a great number of classic works each year.

5. _____ Kansas, _____,
   (is as flat as a tabletop)

   most of Oklahoma is also characterized by vast, level plains.

Putting It Together

Complete the following to create original sentences.

1. Like _____, which _____,
   _____.

2. Unlike _____, who _____, _____
   _____.

3. Like _____, who _____,
   _____.

4. Unlike _____, which _____,
   _____.

One-Word Prepositions: *despite*

Read Explanations 71 and 72, and study the examples. Complete the exercises that follow.

> **Explanation 71:** Use <u>despite</u> to show contrast.
>
> <u>Despite</u> my long hours of studying, I only got a C on the test.
>
> I had to take the job <u>despite</u> the low pay.

Three-Word Prepositions: *in spite of*

> **Explanation 72:** Use <u>in spite of</u> to show contrast.
>
> <u>In spite of</u> my long hours of studying, I only got a C on the test.
>
> I had to take the job <u>in spite of</u> the low pay.

Exercise N5

Change the underlined clauses to phrases using the cues in parentheses and the information in Explanations 71 and 72. Write <u>despite</u> or <u>in spite of</u> in each sentence.

You see: <u>Although the weather forecast was bad</u>, we decided not to call off the jazz festival. (the bad weather forecast)

You write: <u>Despite (or In spite of) the bad weather forecast</u>, we decided not to call off the jazz festival.

1. <u>Although his leg was injured</u>, the soccer player continued to play. *(the injury to his leg)*

   _____, the soccer player continued to play.

2. Herbert lost his job <u>even though he worked hard</u>. *(his hard work)*

   Herbert lost his job _____.

3. <u>Although Jane had a fever of 102 degrees</u>, she insisted on coming to work. *(a 102-degree fever)*

_____, Jane insisted on coming to work.

4. I decided to buy a lottery ticket <u>even though the odds of winning were very poor</u>. *(the very poor odds of winning)*

I decided to buy a lottery ticket _____.

Prepositions that Join Other Words to Act as Adverbs: *on the one hand, on the other hand*

Explanation 73: Use <u>on the one hand</u> before <u>on the other hand</u> to weigh differences.

These two forms are usually used together with a positive and then a negative statement (or a negative and then a positive statement).

On the one hand, <u>+</u>. On the other hand, <u>−</u>.

I'm not sure whether I think this is a good idea. It's difficult to decide for certain.

On the one hand, <u>it could help us earn money right now</u>. On the other hand,
positive element

<u>it could hurt our chances of making money later on</u>.
negative element

On the one hand, <u>−</u>. On the other hand, <u>+</u>.

I'm trying to evaluate Jim as a worker, and I have to weigh pros and cons.

On the one hand, <u>he does work quite slowly</u>. On the other hand,
negative element

<u>he is very accurate and makes few mistakes</u>.
positive element

Exercise N6

Weigh differences by combining the pairs of positive and negative sentences using <u>on the one hand</u> and <u>on the other hand</u>. You may write the negative or positive part first.

Positive Sentence +	Negative Sentence −
He always has something nice to say.	He often interrupts.
It is powerful and smooth riding.	It only gets 12 miles per gallon.
She can make more money out of town.	She would hate to leave her family.
A used machine is much cheaper.	It may not last as long as a new one.

1. I'm not sure what I think of Ronny. _____

   _____

   _____

2. I don't know whether I really want to buy that car. _____

   _____

   _____

3. Gloria is trying to decide whether to take a job out of town. She is weighing the pros and cons. _____

   _____

   _____

4. I can't decide whether to buy a used computer. _____

   _____

   _____

Putting It Together

Part A

Change the underlined clause to a phrase as in the example. Write <u>despite</u> or <u>in spite of</u> in each sentence.

You see: Although he lacked money, Carl was able to get a car.

You write: Despite (In spite of) a lack of money, Carl was able to get a car.

or

<u>Despite (In spite of)</u> lacking money, Carl was able to get a car.

1. <u>Even though they are intelligent</u>, chimpanzees cannot speak.

   _____

2. <u>Although it was snowing heavily</u>, I decided to walk to work.

   _____

3. <u>Although I was in terrible pain</u>, I managed to finish the soccer game.

   _____

4. <u>Although he was fantastically wealthy</u>, Richard had few friends.

   _____

5. <u>Even though he fell more than 40 feet</u>, Paul was not hurt.

   _____

Part B

Complete the following.

1. I'm not sure whether I like _____. On the one hand, _____
   _____. On the other hand, _____
   _____.

2. There are good and bad things with respect to _____. On the one hand, _____
   _____. On the other hand, _____
   _____.

Exercise N7

Complete the dialogue by writing the correct word in each space.

Johnny McKay Shows up on Stage with a Guitar

Larry Gray: How was *Annie Get Your Gun* last night? I couldn't be there.

Doris Pembrose: Oh, I thought I would faint with fright. Really! I nearly passed _____!

1

Larry Gray: What happened?

Doris Pembrose: In the middle of the play, Johnny McKay showed _____ on stage with a guitar!

2

Larry Gray: No!

Doris Pembrose: Yes, and he began to play and sing "Home on the Range" _____ the audience.

3

Larry Gray: Well, at least it was a *western* song. But "Home on the Range" is pretty old and dull, isn't it? And it's not part of the play.

Doris Pembrose: Actually, it wasn't dull _____ all. It was quite different _____ the version I

4   5

am accustomed _____. It was filled with verses and even melodies that I wasn't

6

familiar _____. You know, he stood up there and sang _____ almost ten

7   8

minutes.

Larry Gray: What did the audience do?

Doris Pembrose: Well, of course they thought it was part _____ the play—but they were all

9

_____ the edge of their seats the whole time.

10

Larry Gray: You mean they liked it?

Doris Pembrose: Oh, yes. _____ fact, they loved it! And who wouldn't? It was absolutely

11

beautiful. _____ the end of the song, the audience applauded _____ almost

12   13

a whole minute.

Larry Gray: Still, I'll bet you're mad _____ Johnny.

14

Doris Pembrose: I'm not sure if I'm mad _____ him or not. _____ the one hand, I'm always a
little afraid _____ what crazy thing he might do. _____ the other hand, he is
never really unkind. Despite his weird behavior, he's a pretty nice guy. And I have
never seen a 17-year-old who was as good _____ playing the guitar as he is.

Larry Gray: Well, nice guy or not, I'd kick him _____ the play for what he did.

Doris Pembrose: Are you kidding? The whole town is talking _____ his performance. Half of
the audience is coming _____ again next Saturday just to listen _____ that
one song. I'd be crazy to kick him _____!

Larry Gray: Aren't you even going to talk _____ him?

Doris Pembrose: I already have. I told him I didn't object _____ his song. I only objected
_____ his not telling me first. Then I told him how much I was looking
forward _____ his next performance in the play.

Larry Gray: Boy! You're not mad _____ him _____ all. _____ fact, you sound like
one of his fans!

Doris Pembrose: Well, I have some good reasons to be his fan. _____ one thing, the play is a
fantastic success because _____ him. _____ another thing, I love the way
he sings!

Two-Word Verbs and Multi-Word Verbs: *Take Up, Try Out, Try On, See Off, Take Off*

Read the explanation, and study the examples. Complete the exercises that follow.

Explanation 74: The following is a list of common two-word verbs and their definitions.

Two-Word Verbs	Definitions
take up	start a hobby
try out	try something for the first time
try on	put on a piece of clothing for the first time to see how it looks or how it fits
see off	go to a departure place (an airport, a bus station, etc.) to say good-bye to someone
take off	begin to fly

Exercise N8

Fill in the blanks with the correct two-word verb from Explanation 74. Be sure to write the correct tense or other form of the verb.

1. I got on the plane only minutes before it _____.

2. I just bought a new boat, and I'm looking forward to _____ it _____.

3. I need something to keep me busy. I think I'll _____ gardening.

4. Sid bought new fishing equipment. There was no lake nearby so he _____ it _____ in his family's swimming pool.

5. Pigeons make a loud flapping sound when they _____.

6. Roger Tory Peterson _____ the hobby of bird watching at an early age.

7. That's a nice hat. Why don't you _____ it _____ to see how it looks?

8. These pants are 34/34s. That's my size, but they don't fit. I should have _____ them _____ at the store before I bought them.

9. When I went away to college, my parents went to the airport to _____ me _____.

10. You're leaving for Hawaii? When? I'll _____ you _____ at the airport.

Putting It Together

Answer these questions with a complete sentence using the two-word verbs from Explanation 74.

1. What do you do before you buy clothes?

    _____

2. When a friend is leaving on vacation what do you do?

    _____

3. After you get on a plane, what does it do?

    _____

4. If you want to fill some lonely hours, what can you do?

    _____

5. You have just bought a brand new printer for your computer. What do you do?

    _____

Prepositions in Context

Read this newspaper article about Johnny McKay's invitation to go on tour with Larry and the Locomotives, and answer the questions that follow using the correct prepositions. Write ø if no preposition is needed. Then read the article again to correct your work.

LITTLETOWN DAILY NEWS
Friday, August 27, 2005

Local Boy, Johnny McKay, Gets Big Break
by Brian Cooper

Well, I've written about him more than once, and it seems that this article will not be the last. I'm talking about Littletown's own Johnny McKay, rhythm guitarist, singer, and songwriter. McKay has got his first big break early with an invitation to go on tour with Larry and the Locomotives, a national musical act.

McKay, who took up the guitar only three years ago, has become something of a local celebrity since he first performed at Peabody's Teen Club last year. His rendition of "Home on the Range" in the Littletown High School play *Annie Get Your Gun* brought about even more local interest in this unusually talented 17-year-old. Larry Bender of Larry and the Locomotives found out about McKay from relatives who saw the play.

"This is a big opportunity for Johnny," said Brent Morgan, bass player for McKay's group, Johnny and the Sun Dogs. "The other members of the band and I are really pleased with how things have turned out, and we wish Johnny the best."

Morgan and the other band members never planned to be in the band for good. Instead, they plan to go to college.

So does McKay. Unlike so many other young rockers with big dreams, McKay has a practical attitude with respect to his future. "It doesn't matter who you are. You will be more successful if you graduate from college. So despite my musical plans, I'm going to get a degree someday too," McKay says.

That's not all he will get. Local merchants and others have collected donations for a going-away gift for McKay. It's a Gibson L5 guitar. McKay has always wanted one.

On Saturday, much of Littletown High School will be at the airport to see McKay off and surprise him with the guitar. (I've warned everyone not to let him look at the newspaper until then.)

There won't be enough time for him to try out the new guitar before the plane takes off. However, the Locomotives are scheduled to make several TV appearances in the near future. That means we'll soon see Johnny playing it in our own living rooms. And as usual, you will be reading more about him in my column.

1. Is this the first article Brian Cooper has written about Johnny McKay?

No, he has written _____ him more than once.

2. Has McKay been playing the guitar for many years?

No, he took _____ the guitar only three years ago.

3. How long has he been a local celebrity?

_____ his first performance at Peabody's Teen Club.

4. What caused more local interest in him?

Johnny's version of "Home on the Range" brought _____ even more interest in him.

5. How did Larry Bender learn about Johnny?

He found _____ about Johnny from relatives who saw *Annie Get Your Gun*.

6. What does Brent Morgan say?

He says that it's a big opportunity _____ his friend Johnny. He also says that he and the other members _____ the band are pleased _____ Johnny's success.

7. Did Morgan and the others in the band want to play in the Sun Dogs forever?

No, they didn't want to be in the band _____ good.

8. What do they want to do?

They want to go _____ college.

9. How is Johnny different from other young musicians with dreams?

_____ many other young musicians, he has a practical attitude _____ respect _____ his future.

10. What does Johnny say about his future?

He says that _____ his plans for a musical career, he still wants to graduate _____ college.

11. What have local merchants and others done?

They have bought a gift _____ Johnny. It's a guitar.

12. What happens next Saturday?

Everyone will meet _____ the airport to see Johnny _____ and give him the guitar.

13. Will Johnny read about the surprise before he gets it?

No, Brian Cooper has told everyone not to let Johnny look _____ the newspaper _____ they give him the gift.

14. Will Johnny play the guitar at the airport?

No, there won't be time to try _____ the new guitar before the plane takes _____, but everyone will see Johnny play the new guitar on TV _____ their own living rooms.

15. What does Brian Cooper plan to do?

He plans to write more _____ Johnny McKay in his column.

EXPANSION EXERCISES FOR CHAPTER 7

Complete the following assignments to expand on what you have learned in Chapter 6.

1. Think of four things that you like about your hometown and label them A, B, C, and D. Use the model that follows to write about your hometown. Write more than one sentence about B, C, and D.

My Hometown

There are some good reasons why I like living in my hometown. For one thing, it _____
(A)
That's important to me. For another thing, _____
(B)

_____

_____. My hometown also _____.
(C)
For example, _____
(C)

_____. The _____ in my hometown
(D)
is also quite good. For instance, _____

_____

_____.

Because of all of the above, _____.

2. Write a sentence for each of the two-word verbs in Explanation 74.

3. Think about something that you are unsure about. Then weigh differences using on the one hand and on the other hand.

4. Write sentences using the following sentence structures.

   Unlike, wh _____, _____.

   Example: Unlike Eduardo, who likes to dress up, I prefer to wear casual clothes.

Like, wh _____, _____.

Example: Like Marvin Jones, who graduated with honors, Jennifer Conners finished college at the top of her class.

5. Write sentences using the following sentence structures.

_____. For example, _____.

Example: There are some great places to visit here. For example, the Painted Desert is one of the most famous tourist attractions in the state.

_____. An example is _____.

Example: Some drugs are legal. An example is tobacco.

_____. Some examples are _____.

Example: Many of the people in my class play musical instruments. Some examples are Jim and Maria, who both play the guitar.

6. Combine the following sentences to make one sentence using the preposition of with whom or which. Write whom for people and which for things.

You see: Coming toward us were three men. One of them shouted to me.

You write: Coming toward us were three men, one of whom shouted to me.

a. Michelle won $300. All of it was gone within an hour.

b. I dropped two glasses. Only one of them broke.

c. The gardener planted 30 trees. None of them died.

d. The Bronson family has two cars. Neither of them is big.

e. Herbert has 1,500 books. He has read all of them.

f. We hired three gardeners. Two of them quit within a few days.

COMPREHENSIVE TEST 7

Write the correct word in each space according to what you have learned. If none is needed, write ø in the space.

1. A mouse is similar _____ a rat.

2. Do you know Elk Lake? Well, _____ the north is a campground. See you there!

3. Francis just bought a new sewing machine, and she can't wait to try it _____.

4. Judy's whole family went to the train station to see her _____.

5. I can't decide whether or not to go on the trip. _____ the one hand, I will have a lot of fun. On the other hand, I won't be able to do any of the things I need to do.

6. I chose biology _____ mathematics as a major because it is more interesting to me.

7. I don't like these rules. I object _____ every one of them.

8. I like to collect things. _____ example, I have hundreds of old postcards and more than 1,500 old coins.

9. I took _____ photography last year, but I soon lost interest in it.

10. I tried _____ the hat, but it was too small.

11. I'm _____ having the party downtown because I think it's too far away.

12. Iron is a solid. _____ contrast, hydrogen is a gas.

13. _____ the northwestern part of Manitoba is the shore of Hudson Bay.

14. Many products are made _____ petroleum.

15. My boss insists _____ dedication and hard work from all of his employees.

16. My glasses differ _____ yours in thickness.

17. Napoleon was only five feet, two inches _____ height.

18. _____ the rain, we didn't call the picnic off.

19. The boss gave Donna Dobson a raise because _____ her hard work.

20. The defendant chose to say nothing _____ regard to the charges against him.

21. There are a number of reasons that Mr. Kline is popular. _____ one thing, he is very polite.

22. _____ respect to your request, the answer is yes!

23. There are three bottles on the table, two _____ which are full.

24. While walking in the forest, Henry came _____ an old cabin.

25. Who prefers sadness _____ happiness? No one.

26. With a roar, the jet took _____ and disappeared into the clouds.

27. Yes, I'm familiar with the Conversation Club. _____ fact, I'm the president.

28. _____ insects, which have six legs, spiders have eight.

29. What is missing _____ your life is a hobby. You should take one up.

30. Walk _____ south on Mission Avenue, and then turn right on Elm Street.

ANSWERS TO EXERCISES IN CHAPTER 7

M1: 2. instance or example, got straight As in all of his classes 3. To begin, could start showing up for class regularly 4. instance or example, smokes heavily and never exercises

M2: 2. For instance or For example, also can learn more about our own planet or can also learn more about our own planet 3. For instance or For example, also am the captain of my company's soccer team or am also the captain of my company's soccer team 4. For instance or For example, also put a half gallon of ice cream in the microwave

M3: 1. For one thing, For another thing 2. For one thing, For another thing 3. For one thing, For another thing 4. For one thing, For another thing

M4: 1. Some examples are 2. An example is 3. Some examples are 5. An example is, which once was relatively uncommon. 6. Some examples are, who built hundreds of them. 7. Some examples are, which are sold almost everywhere. 8. An example is, who was perhaps the best of all.

M5: 1–7 of 10. I read three books, two of which were very good. 11. Mack visited four people, all of whom gave him a gift. 12. I have met a lot of teachers, most of whom were very nice. 13. The Bradys took 100 pictures, many of which were just beautiful. 14. The U.S. imports a lot of oil, much of which comes from Saudi Arabia.

M6: 2. In fact, she loves it. 3. In fact, no one can read anything he writes. 4. In fact, it can grow to more than 50 pounds in weight. 5. In fact, they are the largest animals that ever lived.

M7: 1. different from 2. similar to 3. differs from 4. differ from 5. similar to

M8: 2. The planet Jupiter and the planet Mars are different. 3. This city and my hometown differ. 4. Coca-Cola® and Pepsi-Cola® are similar.

M9: 1. in height 2. in width 3. in depth 4. in length 5. in weight

M10: 2. e. 3. c 4. a 5. b 6. f 8. differ in size 9. is different from a square in shape 10. are different in subject 11. differs from sushi in flavor 12. are similar to African deserts in climate 13. are similar in color

M11: 1. with respect to (with/in regard to) your application for the job of office manager 2. with respect to (with/in regard to) his duties as assistant to the superintendent 3. with respect to (with/in regard to) making money

M12: 2. e 3. b 4. c 5. d 7. differ from most people with respect to (with/in regard to) height 8. are different with respect to (with/in regard to) political viewpoint 9. are different with respect to (with/in regard to) smell 10. are almost exactly the same with respect to (with/in regard to) facial features 11. are similar to typewriters with respect to (with/in regard to) use

N1: 1. In contrast 2. In contrast to or As opposed to 3. In contrast to or As opposed to 4. In contrast 5. In contrast to or As opposed to

N2: 2. In contrast to or As opposed to, who is unkind 3. In contrast to or As opposed to, which can be difficult 4. In contrast to or As opposed to, which grows very large

N3: 2. unlike, in or with respect to or with/in regard to 3. In or With respect to or With/In regard to, unlike 4. In or With respect to or With/In regard to, like

N4: 2. Unlike, which is a strong flyer 3. Unlike, which is cold 4. Like, who loves literature 5. Like, which is as flat as a tabletop

N5: 1. Despite (In spite of) the injury to his leg 2. despite (in spite of) his hard work 3. Despite (In spite of) a 102-degree fever 4. despite (in spite of) the very poor odds of winning.

N6: 1. On the one hand, he always has something nice to say. On the other hand, he often interrupts. 2. On the one hand, it is powerful and smooth-riding. On the other hand, it only gets 12 miles per gallon. 3. On the one hand, she can make more money out of town. On the other hand, she would hate to leave her family. 4. On the one hand, a used machine is much cheaper. On the other hand, it may not last as long as a new one. Note: It is also correct to write the negative part first and the positive part second for each of the answers.

N7: 1. out 2. up 3. to 4. at 5. from 6. to 7. with 8. for or ø 9. of 10. at or on 11. In 12. At 13. for or ø 14. at 15. at 16. On 17. of 18. On 19. at 20. out of 21. about 22. back 23. to 24. out 25. to 26. to 27. to 28. to 29. at 30. at 31. In 32. For 33. of 34. For

N8: 1. took off 2. trying, out 3. take up 4. tried, out 5. take off 6. took up 7. try, on 8. tried, on 9. see, off 10. see, off

KEY TO COMPREHENSIVE TESTS

Note: After you find the correct answer to the question and the Explanation(s) that correspond to it, turn to the Contents. It gives you the page number for each Explanation.

Comprehensive Test 1

Answer	Explanation(s)
1. at	5
2. in	1
3. in	1
4. to	5
5. for	6
6. to	6
7. far from	4
8. ∅	7
9. ∅	7
10. ∅	6
11. at	1
12. at	2
13. ∅	7
14. on	2
15. up	8
16. for	8
17. on	2
18. in	2
19. at or on	2
20. in	2
21. on	1
22. off	8
23. near or close to	3 or 4
24. back	8
25. on	8
26. up	8
27. on	2
28. by, beside, next to	3 or 4
29. on	1
30. back	8

Comprehensive Test 2

Answer	Explanation(s)
1. on	9
2. from	15
3. at	9

4.	at	13
5.	to	15
6.	at	9
7.	∅	7 and 8
8.	up	17
9.	to	11
10.	in	9 and 10
11.	beneath, under, underneath or below	14
12.	out	17
13.	in	9 and 10
14.	at	9 and 10
15.	to	15
16.	over or above	14
17.	∅	7
18.	on	17
19.	to	13
20.	at or on	9
21.	on	2
22.	from	10
23.	back	8
24.	from	10
25.	on	9
26.	to	12

27.	in	17
28.	on	17
29.	for	18
30.	at	16

Comprehensive Test 3

Answer		Explanation(s)
1.	of	22
2.	to	20
3.	for	21
4.	by	23
5.	to	20
6.	to	20
7.	on	9
8.	from	15
9.	back	17
10.	from	22
11.	for or ∅	24
12.	for	21
13.	for	21
14.	at	22
15.	at or on	9
16.	since	24

17.	after or subsequent to	23 or 25
18.	of	19
19.	up	26
20.	to	15
21.	up	8
22.	on	9
23.	on	17
24.	at	9
25.	Before or Prior to	23 or 25
26.	off	26
27.	on	26
28.	until	24
29.	at	22
30.	off	26

Comprehensive Test 4

Answer		**Explanation(s)**
1.	on	33
2.	past, beyond	27
3.	prior to, before	23 or 25
4.	to	20
5.	from	10
6.	of	22

7.	on	38
8.	over	37
9.	for	21
10.	away	37
11.	by	32
12.	for	15 and 21
13.	on (exception)	33
14.	up	17
15.	from	36
16.	of	19
17.	in	9
18.	from	15
19.	from	22
20.	in	31
21.	out	37
22.	out	17
23.	catty or kitty corner(ed) to/from	29
24.	from	34
25.	around	27
26.	out	37
27.	over	37
28.	to	37

29. off or out — 37

30. ∅ or to the — 30

Comprehensive Test 5

Answer	Explanation(s)
1. at	46
2. from	15
3. for	6
4. of	48
5. beyond, past, or after	27 or 23
6. at	9
7. from	48
8. for	15 and 21
9. of	19
10. off	8
11. at	22
12. out of	41
13. on or about	45
14. Before or Prior to	23 or 25
15. up	26
16. catty or kitty corner(ed) to/from	29
17. to	47
18. out	40

Answer	Explanation(s)
19. to	42
20. away from	28
21. by	32
22. on	33
23. to	35
24. on	43
25. with	44
26. in	9 and 10
27. ∅	7
28. for	21
29. for or ∅	24
30. of	46

Comprehensive Test 6

Answer	Explanation(s)
1. At	49
2. between	56
3. out	55
4. Among	56
5. on	50
6. to	57
7. up	51
8. on or about	55

9.	over	57
10.	down	51
11.	across or by or upon	55
12.	to	58
13.	to	53
14.	of	58
15.	for or in favor of	59 or 61
16.	on	53
17.	since	24
18.	against or opposed to	59 or 60
19.	to	54
20.	in	52
21.	on	54
22.	on or about	45
23.	up	55
24.	on	17
25.	about	45
26.	at	9
27.	about	55
28.	about	45
29.	for or in favor of	59 or 61
30.	At	49

Comprehensive Test 7

Answer		Explanation(s)
1.	to	64
2.	to	30
3.	out	74
4.	off	74
5.	On	73
6.	over	57
7.	to	53
8.	For	62
9.	up	74
10.	on	74
11.	against or opposed to	59 or 61
12.	In	68
13.	In	31
14.	from	48
15.	on	53
16.	from	65
17.	in	66
18.	Despite or In spite of	71 or 72
19.	of	58
20.	in or with	67

21.	For	62
22.	With	67
23.	of	19
24.	across or by or upon	55
25.	to	57
26.	off	74

27.	In	63
28.	Unlike or In contrast to or As opposed to	69 or 70
29.	from	22
30.	∅ or to the	30